THE
RBG WAY

THE SECRETS OF RUTH BADER GINSBURG'S SUCCESS

REBECCA GIBIAN

Skyhorse Publishing

Skyhorse Publishing books may be purchased in bulk at special discounts for sales promotion, corporate gifts, fund-raising, or educational purposes. Special editions can also be created to specifications. For details, contact the Special Sales Department, Skyhorse Publishing, 307 West 36th Street, 11th Floor, New York, NY 10018 or info@skyhorsepublishing.com.

Skyhorse® and Skyhorse Publishing® are registered trademarks of Skyhorse Publishing, Inc.®, a Delaware corporation.

Visit our website at www.skyhorsepublishing.com.

10 9 8 7 6 5 4 3 2 1

Library of Congress Cataloging-in-Publication Data is available on file.

Cover design by Brian Peterson

ISBN: 978-1-5107-4958-0
Ebook ISBN 978-1-5107-4959-7

Printed in the United States of America

*To the women who dedicate their lives to making the world
a better place for those who follow*

Contents

Introduction

IT IS 1959, AND TWENTY-SIX-YEAR-OLD Ruth Bader Ginsburg is having trouble getting a job. She's already attended Harvard Law School, where she was one of only nine women seated among more than five hundred men.[1] But then her husband, Marty, got a job offer in New York City, so Ginsburg transferred to Columbia Law School, where she became the first woman to be on two major law reviews: the *Harvard Law Review* and *Columbia Law Review*.[2] Now, having graduated from Columbia tied for first in her class, she was looking for a job at a law firm or as a clerk to a judge or justice.

None of her accomplishments seemed to matter to the men in charge of the legal world. She was not given an offer at Paul, Weiss, Rifkind, Wharton & Garrison, despite a successful clerkship the summer before. They already hired an African American woman, which fulfilled their commitment to diversity.[3] Ginsburg applied to a dozen other firms, resulting in only two second interviews and no job offers.[4]

Judge Learned Hand of the US Court of Appeals for the Second Circuit also denied Ginsburg a job, even though they shared an interest in process theory.[5] So did Supreme Court Justice Felix Frankfurter, who wouldn't even interview Ginsburg for a clerkship position.[6]

And there's no question about it: potential employers rejected her due to her gender. Despite graduating at the top of her class, being on two law reviews, and having strong recommendations—including one from a professor (and later dean) at Harvard Law School, Albert Martin Sacks—Ruth Bader Ginsburg was a Jewish woman and a mother to a young toddler, which were three strikes against her. She may have accomplished a lot, on top of seeing her husband through his first bout of cancer, but she just couldn't get a job.

★ ★ ★

Let's jump forward to 2018, when I, a twenty-seven-year-old journalist, am eating cheesecake from a box and drinking rosé out of a thermos my roommate and I smuggled into a crowded movie theater in Brooklyn, watching a documentary on the now-notorious RBG. Not only did she find a job, but since ascending to the highest court in the land, Ruth Bader Ginsburg has become a cult icon for feminism and equality, thanks to the way she fundamentally changed American law surrounding gender bias and gender equality, and thanks to the ringing dissents she has started reading from the bench as the court has become more and more conservative. There are T-shirts, candles, coffee mugs, tote bags, and travel cups with her face on them. There has been a multitude of books about her life as a pioneer of gender equality and the law. There is an opera about her friendship with the late Justice Antonin Scalia, there are awards in her honor, there is a Tumblr blog dedicated to her, and tattoos of her quotes or her face adorn people's bodies. She's been called the "Thurgood Marshall of the women's movement"[7] and the "most important woman lawyer in the history of the Republic."[8] Ruth Bader Ginsburg not only changed the laws in this country, legally shrinking the divide between men and women, but she has inspired both women and men to speak up and dissent when they encounter inequality or injustice, to fight hard for whatever they believe in. She stayed true to her lifelong message: no separate categories for genders.[9]

I have long admired Ruth Bader Ginsburg—as shown through the candle holder and mug with her likeness on them that were gifted to me long before I started writing this book. In fact, she was so frequently a topic of inspiration and conversation among one group of friends when we lived together in Washington, DC, that no one was surprised when our smallest housemate, a young kitten, was named Ruth Bader Ginsburg (we called her Ruthie B. for short).

But last year, while sitting in the borough where RBG was born, watching her on the big screen, I wondered if there was a way for people to follow in her footsteps, no matter their career, instead of purely idolizing her. So when, a few months later, Skyhorse Publishing asked me if I would be interested in writing a book about RBG's pathway to success, it felt like someone had been reading my thoughts.

When I agreed to do this book, I knew that there were already many fantastic, well-researched, and in-depth biographies written that describe Justice Ginsburg's life, cases, and relationships, and I in no way wish to encroach on that territory. As the justice always says, I stand on the shoulders of those who came before me. Instead, this book explores the idea that there are lessons we can all take away from RBG's life and apply to our own lives to maybe become a little more successful in our relationships and careers and efforts to create change.

I spent months reading every book, article, and think piece about Ruth Bader Ginsburg that I could, as well as reading her own briefs, dissents, speeches, and talks. I watched the documentary and movie made about her life and listened to her give interviews and talks (I have seen her speak twice in person, once with the late Justice Antonin Scalia in February 2014, when the two discussed press freedoms as part of *The Kalb Report*. And then once in December 2018, with NPR's legal affairs correspondent Nina Totenberg). I also conducted nearly twenty interviews of Ginsburg's former law clerks, colleagues, journalists, and friends, and spoke to some of the authors who have written the biographies and books I mentioned above. While I did reach out to the justice herself multiple times, I was told via her assistant that the justice "appreciates my interest," but politely declined my request to be interviewed. In all honesty, this was unsurprising; the same day I received that email, the Notorious RBG was the sole dissenter on an abortion case that had been heard by the Supreme Court that Term. As author Jane De Hart did in the preface to her extensive Ruth Bader Ginsburg biography, I will quote legal analyst Jeffrey Rosen in saying Justice Ginsburg is "always everywhere and just out of reach."[10]

The research and interviews I did focus on Ruth Bader Ginsburg's way of life—regarding what she has done, the relationships she has cultivated, and the advice she gives—with the goal of maybe giving people direct takeaways that they can use within their own lives. Throughout this book, I will reference Justice Ginsburg's own words and work, the research and books written by others, and the conversations that I had with those who know her better than me, and I will do my best to explain when a source said something directly to me, or wrote/said it elsewhere. The book is split into three sections and includes nine chapters total, because in full cheesiness, there are three branches of government and the Supreme Court is made up of nine justices (I know; I'm sorry).

Of course, there is no way to fully reenact or encompass RBG's existence, but there are plenty of lessons to learn from her partnerships, her dissents, her humor, and more.

Who doesn't want to be a little more notorious in their own life?

PART I
Fighting for Equality

"We should not be held back from pursuing our full talents, from contributing what we could contribute to the society, because we fit into a certain mold, because we belong to a group that historically has been the object of discrimination."

—Ruth Bader Ginsburg, during a 2001 interview[1]

1

On When There Are Nine

RUTH BADER GINSBURG'S STOMACH FILLED with butterflies as she adjusted the microphone in front of her. The lawyer felt nauseous all morning on that cold day. Still, she managed to complete her usual exercise routine, one that she took out of the Canadian Air Force Exercise Manual, before donning her mother's jewelry and making her way to 1 First Street NE in Washington, DC.[1] That day, January 17, 1973, marked the first time the Rutgers University law professor stood in front of the nine male justices of the Supreme Court, hoping to convince them that the archaic laws that discriminated on the basis of sex were both unfair and "senseless."[2] She had ten minutes.

Ginsburg was arguing on behalf of a female Air Force lieutenant in *Frontiero v. Richardson,* a case that highlighted how women in the military were not granted the same guarantees regarding compensation that were given to male service members.[3] But the case was also a stepping-stone for Ginsburg on her path to showing the highest court in the land that women's rights are human rights and that gender discrimination in the law needs to change.

The less-than-one-hundred-pound lawyer[4] cleared her throat and in a confident, calm voice, stated her case. Before she concluded, Ginsburg quoted from abolitionist and feminist Sarah Grimké, "I ask no favor for my sex. All I ask of our brethren is that they take their feet off our necks."[5] Remarkably, the room remained profoundly silent and not a single justice interrupted her to ask a question.[6]

The outcome of Ginsburg's first Supreme Court appearance was the court's most important and far-reaching decision on sex discrimination in history,[7] but for the future justice, it was just one step in a lifelong battle toward gender equality in the nation and the law.

★ ★ ★

RBG changed the way the world is for American women,[8] as legal correspondent Nina Totenberg put it in the *RBG* documentary, because she has an incredible work ethic and a deep passion for the law and the people she's fighting for. As a lawyer, she crafted a plan that slowly and methodically knocked down discriminatory standards. When faced with obstacles, she never got angry but instead adjusted her strategy and kept pushing forward. She is a pure embodiment of the idea that hard work pays off.

I am going to start off this book by offering an overview of how Ruth Bader Ginsburg got to the point of radically affecting Americans' lives, and examine all the ingredients it takes to make a person as successful, tenacious, dedicated, and kind as she is. There is so much to learn from her, and I will focus on specific lessons in the following chapters, but I want to start by giving you an understanding of Ginsburg's overall career trajectory.

For starters, RBG did not originally set out to correct decades' worth of laws based on stereotypes. Her interest in law was ignited by a constitutional scholar and writer on civil liberties at Cornell, Robert Cushman, who was the first person to encourage her to go to law school. In college he supervised Ruth's independent studies project and hired her as his assistant.[9] Ginsburg called Cushman both a "teacher and a consciousness raiser."[10] He assigned Ginsburg a research project on Joseph McCarthy's practices so that she would understand the nation was betraying its most fundamental values and learn that legal skills could challenge what was happening and maybe even make things better.[11] While working with Cushman, the future justice realized that she could be a lawyer and help repair problems in her community and the nation.[12]

As we go through the lessons we can learn from Ginsburg's fight for women's rights, it is important to note she was in her forties the first time she argued in front of the Supreme Court and wasn't nominated to the bench until she was sixty. Some people know what they want to do from an early age, some people figure it out in college, and others figure it out after they've had an entirely separate career.

Though RBG went into law because of her drive and dedication to helping people, she probably could have happily taught courses on civil procedure for the rest of her life. Instead, a simple request for help from female students at

Rutgers changed the course of Ginsburg's career. Her later commitment to women's rights resulted from a dedication to equality for all marginalized people.[13]

You should never be afraid to pursue what you love, even if it means taking on new challenges. But the other lessons that we can learn—always turning in your best work, knowing your audience, not giving in to anger—these are skills and traits RBG used her whole life, whether it was in school, or as a professor, then litigator, then judge.

★ ★ ★

In order to fully understand the impact that Ruth Bader Ginsburg has had on women's equality in the law, we need to understand what the legal environment looked like for women when she first got started.

"You have to go back and recapture just how novel what she was trying to do was when she tried to do it and it was unclear what was going to work," said Joan Williams, a professor at the UC Hastings College of the Law who has played a central role in reshaping the conversation about work, gender, and class.

As a student at Cornell, RBG used to hide in the bathroom (and therefore hide her intelligence) in order to do her coursework.[14] When Ginsburg entered law school in 1965, women made up less than 3 percent of the legal profession in the United States, and only one woman had ever served on a federal appellate court.[15] Women were so rare in law schools that the dean of Harvard Law, Erwin Griswold, had all the women over to his house for dinner and asked them how they justified "taking a spot from a qualified man."[16] From 1947 until 1967, women filled between 3 and 4½ percent of the seats in law school each academic semester.[17] As it is well documented, Ginsburg joined the faculty of Rutgers University in 1963. At the time of her appointment, fewer than twenty women were headed for tenure at schools belonging to the Association of American Law Schools.[18]

The law itself also looked very different. There was no legal concept of martial rape.[19] "Sex discrimination claims were simply not taken seriously by the US Supreme Court before 1970," write lawyers Elizabeth Schneider and Stephanie Wildman in their book, *Women and the Law.* "And not many sex discrimination cases even reached the Supreme Court prior to 1970."[20]

Women couldn't serve on juries in all fifty states until 1975,[21] and it wasn't until 1976 that the first group of women was admitted into a US military academy.[22] Before 1974, single or divorced females who wanted to apply for a credit card were often required to bring in a male to cosign their application.[23] (Women faced a similar situation when trying to rent an apartment[24]). And of course, pregnant women faced discrimination at work. Ginsburg herself was told she wasn't eligible for a promotion when she was pregnant with her first child and therefore later hid her second pregnancy from her employers at Rutgers for fear she would not get tenure.[25] Until the 1978 Pregnancy Discrimination Act was passed, employers were under no obligation to keep workers who got pregnant.[26]

Looking back now, it seems remarkable how different the landscape was for women just over forty years ago. And we have Ginsburg to thank for many of those changes (she helped draft the Pregnancy Discrimination Act[27] and served as the attorney representing Marsha Healy in opposing Louisiana's optional jury service for women,[28] to name just two of her many accomplishments).

Women of course can now rent apartments on their own, get credit cards, serve on juries, join any branch of the military, and much more. The year 2016 marked the first time that women made up the majority of US law students, holding just over 50 percent of the seats at accredited law schools in the country.[29] More than one in three lawyers (38 percent) are now women.[30]

"A system of justice will be the richer for diversity of background and experience," Ginsburg once said. "It will be poorer, in terms of appreciating what is at stake and the impact of its judgments, if all of its members are cast from the same mold."[31]

While these accomplishments are great, to put it lightly, Justice Ginsburg would likely agree that there is still a long way to go.

★ ★ ★

Since it is hard to keep track of all the roles RBG has played, I want to give a quick rundown. This in no way encapsulates every case, dissent, project, or accomplishment that she has taken part in in terms of women's equality, but I hope it is enough to give a glimpse of the power Ruth Bader Ginsburg has wielded over gender discrimination in the law.

"She had kind of three periods, one was sort of the firebrand litigator, but very careful and methodical and strategic litigator, and then one was kind of the lawyer's lawyer on the Supreme Court, and now she has this cultural icon figure, culture icon status," said Williams. "She's had a very different persona over the course of her career."

Remember back in the introduction of this book, where young Ginsburg was having trouble getting a job? Well, as you might know, she got one, as a judicial clerk to Judge Edmund Palmieri, US District Court of the Southern District of New York. After that, she worked as a research associate and then associate director of Columbia Law School (this was from 1961–1963).[32] During this period, she divided her time between New York and Sweden, as she was working on a project on International Procedure. It was here that she started to think seriously about women's equality after being exposed to Swedish law.[33] In 1963, she became a professor at Rutgers School of Law.[34] This is where students approached her to ask her to teach a course on sex discrimination.

This seemingly innocuous request ended up propelling Ginsburg into a life that she may never have expected. Frank Askin, Ginsburg's former colleague at both Rutgers and the ACLU, said that in the late 1960s, Ginsburg was "essentially a quiet, retiring scholar of civil procedure and comparative law" whose biggest writing at the time was a book on Swedish civil procedure. But then, something "transformed her," Askin, now retired and speaking to me from Florida, told me. Female students at Rutgers needed a mentor, he explained, and since there were only two women on the Rutgers faculty at the time, they approached Ginsburg.

"And basically, (the students) became Ruth's mentor," Askin said. "And they transformed her into a feminist. She started teaching, you know, feminism and the law, they convinced her to start taking cases and they would help her with the cases, and suddenly she was transformed from this very shy, retiring scholar into an ardent, feminist lawyer, and the rest is history. That's the story."

One of those women, Elizabeth Langer, once said that initially she was surprised Ginsburg was willing to do it.

"She went where other people wouldn't go. She took a leap," Langer told *Rutgers News*. "Once she came on board, everything fell into place. We felt empowered."[35]

Langer said Ginsburg is "an amazingly smart, dedicated, and focused legal mind."[36]

Professor Ginsburg leapt into her new role by reading every federal decision ever published involving women's legal status. She also read every law review article on the topic. It didn't take her very long, as there were not many decisions yet focused on sex discrimination, and very little commentary written thus far.[37]

Reading every federal decision invigorated Ginsburg, and she started to question how people had been putting up with these decisions, but more importantly, how she personally had been dealing with them.[38]

But when Ginsburg started teaching these courses, she had yet to define herself as a feminist. In fact, it wasn't until she read Simone de Beauvoir's *The Second Sex* that RBG really understood and appreciated the feminist ideology.[39] RBG was so affected by the book—which presented concepts of sex, sexual difference, and internalized oppression in a way Ginsburg had not thought of before[40]—that Ruth crawled into bed and read parts of it out loud to her daughter.[41]

"We see her as a mentor, a heroine, a very strong perseverant figure in the women's rights movement," Langer said in an interview with *Rutgers News*. "She had step-by-step strategies to advance the movement."[42]

In 1972, Ginsburg started working at the ACLU, where she founded the Women's Rights Project—she promptly put up a sign at the office that said "Women Working"[43] in their office. She went on to successfully argue five cases before the Supreme Court, all focused on laws and government policies that were built on gender stereotypes (it is important to note she argued six cases total in front of the court, losing one).

Now, her time at the Women's Rights Project is where Ginsburg's keen strategic eye and slow, methodical approach to changing the law come into play. She wanted to discredit perpetual gender stereotypes of men and women's roles in society[44] and believed that many lawmakers saw laws that discriminate on the basis of gender as ways to help women or safeguard them from the hardships of the world.

"Gender classifications were always rationalized as favors to women," Ginsburg can be heard saying during an episode of *Radiolab*.[45]

In order to combat this train of thought, Ginsburg wanted to get sex discrimination recognized by the law the same way race discrimination was recognized.

"During the 1970s, she was trying to establish that the standard of review for an equal protection challenge based on sex discrimination should be the same standard as the court applied to race discrimination, which in legalese is called strict scrutiny," Lenora Lapidus, the late executive director of the ACLU's Women's Rights Project, explained to me on the phone. (Sadly, Lapidus died from breast cancer a few months after we spoke.)

As Ginsburg was working toward this goal, the Equal Rights Amendment was being ratified and debated in the states. Several Supreme Court justices were reluctant to establish this highest level of scrutiny out of concern that it would preempt the political process. Many justices thought the ERA was going to be ratified, Lapidus told me, and that "would answer the question through a political mechanism rather than the courts coming out ahead of the people."

During this time, when Ginsburg would try to talk about sex-based discrimination to men, many often responded with, essentially, "Why are women complaining?" People believed that in fact, women were treated better than men, because they could decide to work or not, they could decline sitting on a jury if they were selected, they could enlist in the military or they could avoid service. So what's the issue?[46] This reaction is what Ginsburg and her team at ACLU were trying to disprove. They were working instead to "educate, along with the public, decisionmakers in the nation's legislatures and courts."[47]

Ginsburg once explained her team's goals, saying, "We tried to convey to them that something was wrong with their perception of the world." As Justice Brennan wrote in a 1973 Supreme Court plurality opinion, *Frontiero v. Richardson*, decided a year and a half after the court had begun to listen: "Traditionally, [differential treatment on the basis of sex] was rationalized by an attitude of 'romantic paternalism' which, in practical effect put women, not on a pedestal, but in a cage."[48]

She specifically chose the ACLU to fight this battle, instead of an organization with a narrower women's rights agenda, because she believed the organization "would enhance the credibility of the women's rights cause"[49] and because she "wanted to be a part of a general human rights agenda . . . [promoting] the equality of all people and the ability to be free."[50]

However, the ERA was not ratified, and the Supreme Court never adopted strict scrutiny. But thanks to Ginsburg's careful choosing of cases, and later her actions once on the Supreme Court, Lapidus said to me that "for all intents and purposes, we are basically at strict scrutiny, but maybe one slight step below."

A Quick Look at Ginsburg's Important ACLU Cases During the 1970s[51]

Reed v. Reed: Ginsburg wrote a brief for this case. The court ruled for the first time that a law that discriminates against women is unconstitutional under the Fourteenth Amendment.

Frontiero v. Richardson: Ginsburg argued this case, in which the Supreme Court struck down a federal statute that gave male members of the armed forces housing and benefits for their wives, but required female members to show the "actual dependency" of their husbands in order to get the same benefits.

Weinberger v. Weisenfeld: Ginsburg, who said this case was "near and dear to her heart,"[52] argued on behalf of Stephen Weisenfeld. She successfully proved that a provision of the Social Security Act that allowed for sex-based distinctions in the awarding of Social Security benefits was unconstitutional.

Craig v. Boren: The court finally adopts a "heightened scrutiny" standard of review to evaluate legal distinctions on the basis of sex, which means that a sex-based legal distinction must bear a substantial relationship to an important governmental interest. Ginsburg worked closely with the lawyer on this case and authored an amicus brief.

Califano v. Goldfarb: Ginsburg argued this case, and the court invalidated sex-based distinctions in the payment of Social Security survivor benefits, because these distinctions were based in archaic assumptions about women's dependency.

In order to get to a point one step below strict scrutiny, Ginsburg took a slow approach. Instead of making sweeping changes to the law, she decided litigators needed to go after the "insidious idea that the Supreme Court had been keeping alive for years," WYNC's Julia Longoria explained expertly in the *Radiolab* episode "Sex Appeal," "that discrimination is actually good for women."[53]

So, while RBG did take on female plaintiffs, a big part of her approach was to bring cases where males were the victims. *Radiolab's* explanation of this strategy puts it really well: In this sense, Ginsburg's strategy was "like a Trojan horse"[54] because on the outside, these cases appeared to be situations where men were being discriminated against, but instead, it's a case against the "unspoken idea" that women need protection from "scary places like bars or courtrooms or political office."[55]

Unsurprisingly, Ginsburg faced criticism for appearing to ignore some issues that were important to the feminist movement. But she said that not all feminist issues could be litigated right away, because given the political climate, some of those cases would lose in court. This would set back the group's efforts to develop an equal standard for all sexes.[56] Those issues would see their time in the sun eventually, Ginsburg believed, but the country needed to be ready.

★ ★ ★

"She cares, it's hard for me to stress in words, the passion she feels, and you can see it in her when she gets aroused, the passion in her for equal rights for women," said Marvin Kalb, a journalist, writer, and acquaintance of Ginsburg's. "The idea that [women], I think I read recently, get 79 cents for every dollar a man gets, that infuriates her, and she's determined to push with everything that she still has in her, to take care of that and to get some legal underpinning for gender equality."

Ginsburg worked as hard as she did because of this passion. In 1975, she argued a case before the Supreme Court in the morning (*Weinberger v. Weisenfeld*) and then rushed back to New York in order to teach her two o'clock class.[57] She still loves the law to this day—she has said having a seat on the Supreme Court is "the best and most consuming job a lawyer anywhere could have."[58]

But her passion extends beyond just the law; Ginsburg truly, deeply cares for the people she is representing, and frequently reminds her clerks that real people are affected by the work they're doing. She has a "real passion and genuine heartfelt caring for the clients, the plaintiffs in the cases," said Lapidus.

A great representation of this is exemplified by Ginsburg's long-held friendship with Stephen Wiesenfeld, the plaintiff from one of her early ACLU cases, *Weinberger v. Wiesenfeld*. Wiesenfeld became a widower after his wife, Paula, died in childbirth. He wanted to care for his son, so Wiesenfeld cut his hours and looked for child care. He tried to apply for Social Security survivors' benefits, only to find they were available for widows but not widowers. Ginsburg and Melvin Wulf, an ACLU colleague, took on the case. The section of the Social Security Act was deemed unconstitutional.[59]

Ginsburg loved what this case did in that it provided the groundwork for future gender discrimination cases and loved what Wiesenfeld was fighting for, the ability to take care of his son in the way that a woman would. His case "contradicted the traditional roles of men as breadwinners and women as caregivers," wrote journalist Robert Barnes in the *Washington Post*.[60]

"There can be incentives and encouragement, but women will have achieved true equality when men share with them the responsibility of bringing up the next generation," Ginsburg said in an interview for a 2001 issue of *The Record*.[61]

However, Ginsburg also cared deeply for Stephen and his son, Jason, with whom she's kept in touch over the years. In fact, Ginsburg helped edit Jason's application essay to Columbia Law School[62] and the justice even presided over his wedding in 1998. When Jason was diagnosed with cancer in his twenties, Ginsburg was there to tell him how she and Marty overcame the disease themselves and assured him that this too would pass.[63] Happily, Jason did recover, and RBG later officiated Stephen's wedding four decades after their case, in 2014.[64]

Lapidus really hammered this point home when she said of RBG, "Although she's brilliant and has the legal arguments at the epitome of the legal argumentation, it's really about the people and their lives and what is the impact that this law or practice have and how can her decisions really make a difference in their lives on the ground."

The takeaway for the rest of us from this attitude is an important one: Our actions affect other people in both big and small ways. No matter what career path you chose, keep in mind that the things you do will reverberate through the community you are in.

★ ★ ★

Ginsburg knew her pathway forward and, as a litigator, had a plan she believed would work, even though it was criticized by some. She was a genius when it came to strategy, which is clear from the cases she picked and the way she chipped away at gender discrimination in the law. Ginsburg obviously did not have total control over the cases that would be heard by the Supreme Court, but she worked hard to represent clients and cases that would go against the anachronistic line of thinking that laws that discriminate on the basis of gender are there to help and protect women.

Although she had a strategic method, things did not always go her way, and Ginsburg's plan was not always successful. We also know from her dissents that since getting on the Supreme Court, Ginsburg has not always gotten her way while on the bench. Through it all, the justice can adapt and has done so, Jane De Hart, author of *Ruth Bader Ginsburg: A Life*, emphasized during our phone interview. When best-laid plans go awry, Ginsburg figures out a way around the problem.

Former clerk Richard Primus, during an interview with the University of Michigan (where he is now a professor), said while clerking for RBG, he learned the importance of seeing the big picture while doing small things within the law. She also taught him to avoid making a new mess while fixing something else.

"I was working on a cert petition where there was an issue about jury instructions. It was clear to me that the jury instructions had gone wrong, and the justice didn't disagree with me about that," he said. Ginsburg took him through and explained they would be better off living with the problem until there was a clear plan to fix the other problems coming down the pipeline.[65]

Primus, who called Ginsburg a "cautious crusader," went on to say this was a really valuable lesson for him to learn. Many people forget to keep the big picture in mind while sweating the small stuff, but Ginsburg keeps it firmly in focus.[66]

"Well, one thing is that you never give up. You keep fighting," said Kalb, when asked what people should learn from Ginsburg's life. He chuckled before saying that Ginsburg will always continue the battle, "because it has not yet been won. And the idea is that you don't give up; you keep fighting for what you believe in."

★ ★ ★

An integral part of her strategic approach and her fight for the cause was knowing her audience. As Williams put it to me, RBG knew that she would be talking to "basically eight white guys and Justice Marshall." So, she started with the end in mind when she argued in front of the Supreme Court.

"She tried to frame the issue of gender discrimination in a way that they could hear and understand it," Williams said.

"And she did that while retaining quite a radical edge, so she used language of subordination, which is language that is so edgy that we hardly even use it anymore, but she combined it with strategies like showing how gender roles disadvantage men, and switching the terminology from sex discrimination to gender discrimination because she didn't want to be talking to nine men about sex and have their minds go in quite a different direction than she intended."

For example, in the brief that Ginsburg wrote for *Reed v. Reed*, she uses the terms "inferior," "subordinate," "subordination," and "second-class" fifteen times.[67] Williams once wrote in an essay that Ginsburg was focused on "reconstructing gender."[68] She wanted to get rid of the idea that there were men's roles and women's roles, and create a society where women could gain access to positions typically held by men and vice versa.[69]

"She also just had the raw intelligence to understand the idea that gender is a hierarchy in which women are subordinated is not inconsistent with the idea that gender roles hurt men as well as women," Williams explained to me during our interview. "Most people assume those two are mutually exclusive, but of course they're not."

A lesser-known example of Ginsburg's intellectual use of subordination language can be seen in the brief for *Struck v. Secretary of Defense*. This brief is not as widely known as others, because the Supreme Court ultimately declined to hear the case, but Ginsburg was writing on behalf of an Air Force officer, Captain Susan Struck. She got pregnant in 1970 while serving in Vietnam and was given two options: have a legal abortion on the Air Force base or leave the military. Struck tried to explain that she disagreed with abortion on religious grounds but was planning to give the child up for adoption after she gave birth. However, Struck was still forced to leave the military. Ultimately, the military changed its policy, so the case was never heard.[70]

Before it was dismissed, Ginsburg wrote a brief explaining that laws enforcing traditional sex stereotypes are harmful because they add to "the subordinate position of women in our society and the second-class status our institutions historically have imposed upon them."[71]

One of Ginsburg's ultimate goals during the 1970s was to challenge laws that enforced traditional sex-role stereotypes because they classify women as having a lower status than men.[72] She believed that laws like this "violated equal protection because they denied individual women equal opportunity."[73] Thanks to Ginsburg, many on the court have now adopted this line of thinking.[74]

★ ★ ★

On top of knowing that her audience was mainly older white men, who in their own heads were good fathers and husbands, Ginsburg also knew how to craft an argument that they would listen to. Instead of fighting or yelling, Ginsburg would persuade.

"Principally what she was doing was this act of translation, making her reality and the reality of women's lived experience visible to men who were quite certain that they were not sexist, they were just good protectors," said Dahlia Lithwick, a journalist who writes about law and politics in the United States and has interviewed Ginsburg multiple times. And though some people may think this happened a hundred thousand years ago, in reality, these ideas and laws existed just a few decades ago. So while Ginsburg's approach may seem old-fashioned or not nearly radical enough, Lithwick thinks RBG "was making a very careful calculation about what would be radical but what would in a sense demand empathy from men who thought they were already perfectly sympathetic."

For example, in an amicus brief filed in *Frontiero v. Richardson,* Ginsburg wrote that women who want to participate in jobs or roles outside of what seen as stereotypically female do not want to be protected. What they want, instead, is to not be confined by classifications about traditional male and female roles. Legislation should not stop people from reaching their full potential even when household gender roles deviate from the norm, as they did in *Frontiero.* Her brief reiterated the idea that decision-making bodies made up of only men were holding on to ideas that did not protect, but instead hurt, women.[75]

Ginsburg used facts over anger when in front of her all-male audience. She knew that she, a small, quiet woman, would be facing nine men who believed that they were caring husbands, fathers, feminists. She knew in order to win she had to have the facts laid out in a reasonable way, and that anger wouldn't work. Of course, it is important to note that by temperament, Ginsburg is not a loud or angry person. Lithwick explained to me that Ginsburg felt that "she stood on the shoulders of other women who had gone storming into court and said, 'You guys are sexist pigs,' and never prevailed." Knowing what didn't work allowed Ginsburg to be pragmatic about her approach.

"I think, in a strange way, what she had to do was convince [the men on the court] that their altruism [was] wrong, and that's sort of a double load," said Lithwick. "On the one hand, you're basically saying that you think you're giving [women] freedom but you're in fact just putting them in a cage and that's a really, really hard thing because it has to pierce this false confidence of being a good father, a good provider, a good spouse, a supportive spouse." The way Ginsburg had to make this "unbelievably heavy lift" was essentially by saying to the men, "You're not in bad faith, but imagine if this was done to you, imagine if the stereotypes about your capacity or your values were foisted upon you against your will."

Ginsburg does not allow herself to get sucked into the allure of outrage, explained Elizabeth Porter, who clerked for the justice in 2002–2003. Instead, Ginsburg focuses on what is important, and prioritizes things that matter. Doing this requires more than just working long hours, but also needs a "supportive environment and a solid education," Porter elaborated in an email to me.

"I think young people who would like to emulate Justice Ginsburg should focus on creating healthy friendships, finding a life partner who is emotionally intelligent and secure, finding educational opportunities to learn critical thinking, and aiming toward long-term goals rather than getting caught up in the outrage du jour (of which there will always be plenty)," she said.

★ ★ ★

During her time at the ACLU, Ginsburg submitted briefs in twenty-four Supreme Court cases—many that had resounding impact on gender equality—and appeared before the court to present oral argument in six cases. Through these cases and briefs, Ginsburg crafted the legal arguments that were then seen in the court's opinions. Her role earned her the honorific title of the "Thurgood Marshall of the women's movement."[76]

Following her time running the Women's Rights Project, Ginsburg was hired in 1972 as the first tenured female law professor in Columbia University Law School's 114-year history.[77] That year, with help from Professors Herma Hill Kay of the University of California Berkeley law school and Kenneth Davidson of the State University of New York at Buffalo, Ginsburg created a casebook on sex discrimination and law. Ginsburg also used her position of power to help others, both at Columbia and Rutgers. When she became the first tenured female professor at Columbia Law School, people immediately began airing grievances, such as how employees didn't have pregnancy coverage, how women got lower pension benefits and lower pay, and how the university was about to lay off more than two dozen maids, all women, but not any male janitors.[78] In response, Ginsburg filed a class action lawsuit, she wrote to Columbia's president, and she got the New York branch of the ACLU involved. She was tenured, so her job was not directly at risk, but her reputation at the school was.[79]

Over the next decade, Ginsburg wrote more than twenty-five legal articles about law and gender equality. By the time she was hired as a judge of the US Court of Appeals for the DC Circuit in 1980, state and federal law had been revolutionized and looked radically different. She spent thirteen years on the bench in DC before becoming the second woman nominated to the Supreme Court of the United States of America.[80]

Of course, during her time as a justice she has only continued her life's work. Since taking her seat in 1993, Ginsburg has authored nearly two hundred opinions.[81] Her dissents are legendary, but she has also authored or been behind important majority opinions. For example, during her third term on the Supreme Court, Ginsburg authored the majority opinion in *United States v. Virginia* on behalf of six members of the court (better known as the *VMI* case). This decision fortified the court's approach to gender equality, which had developed in large part thanks to Ginsburg's work in the 1970s.[82]

And she's not done fighting yet.

She is frequently asked when there will be enough women on the Supreme Court. Her response? "When there are nine." (She repeated her desire for an all-female Court when I saw her speak this past December). The justice says people are shocked by this answer, but no one has "ever raised a question" about nine men serving on the bench.[83]

★ ★ ★

Ginsburg is proof that working hard and turning in your best work actually does pay off. In fact, "best work" was a phrase that the justice used to use a lot, according to Margo Schlanger, one of Ginsburg's first Supreme Court clerks.

You can have enough passion that you feel fit to burst, but actually putting your head down and doing the work is different. Ruth Bader Ginsburg's work ethic is legendary— her late hours and lack of sleep date back to when she and her husband were in law school—but more importantly, the work she completed was good, thorough, and well-done.

"Those people who care about the things they do want to do them right and do them well," said former clerk Goodwin Liu, now an Associate Justice on the Supreme Court of California.

Aryeh Neier, the former executive director of the ACLU who brought Ginsburg on to the organization, once wrote that it was a "sheer pleasure" to read her briefs.

"They were simply superb pieces of legal argumentation," he wrote in an essay honoring Ginsburg's twenty-fifth anniversary on the court. Neier said her briefs also represented her personality: Spare. "The briefs were tough in their language, and you couldn't slip a knife between the arguments. They were so tightly reasoned."[84]

People who want to learn from the Notorious RBG should learn that "words matter" and to have a "professional attitude towards your work," said David Post, who twice clerked for Ginsburg, once on the DC Circuit and again when she became a justice. If something was going out under her name, "she was going to make it as perfect as it could be."

The Notorious RBG authors tell a story about how RBG's clerks, at the end of one term, gave the justice a menu as a gift, but basically every word on the menu was changed, as a reflection of the justice's editing style.[85]

"I think she definitely was one of these people who grew up in an era where she had to be twice as good to get half as far," said Justice Liu. "And so, she just developed a habit of making sure that everything she did was extremely high quality and could not ever be questioned and that has carried her throughout her whole life."

Ginsburg wasn't just working long hours to rack up hours; she truly wanted to produce her best work, explained Schlanger.

"[One] thing that I learned from working for her is that every single piece of work product that you're producing, every single piece of work that you produce for someone else, should represent your best work, that there should be no throwaways," said Schlanger. "If you're handing somebody a piece of work, and saying, 'I think you should use this,' then it should be your best work."

Another clerk, Sam Bagenstos (also Schlanger's husband), is now a professor at the University of Michigan Law School. When asked by the school what adjectives he would use to describe Ginsburg, he first stated that the justice does not believe in adjectives. Instead, she believes that one can be most expressive through verbs and nouns. He went on to call her an "incredibly warm and generous person."[86]

This work ethic and dedication also lends itself to Ginsburg being incredibly reliable. You know that person in the group project who says they'll do sections two and three, but when you meet to talk it over, conveniently just had a really busy week and didn't get it done? Ruth Bader Ginsburg would never be that person.

"I never heard anybody say, 'Oh, we were counting on Ruth and she didn't come through,' never," said Barbara Babcock, another early pioneer of women's equality and the law.

Another thing about Ginsburg's work ethic is that she figured out what worked for her. For example, we've all heard about her intense work hours (and very little sleep). She is not a morning person, explained Post, and so she does not work in the morning (unless court is in session).

"She knew when and how she worked best, and she was in a position to make sure she worked during that time and so she did," Post explained. He often jokes with his wife, another non–morning person, that she should be more like RBG and refuse to go to breakfast meetings.

I feel this on a deeply personal level, as someone who also hates mornings and works better later in the day. So the lesson that I am taking from this is never to do anything before 11 a.m., because that's how RBG would want it. (Just kidding, future bosses.) In all seriousness, it is important to learn how and when you work best so that you can turn in the best possible product, every time.

★ ★ ★

It's hard to imagine emulating all the traits we just went through.

"She's a very interesting blend of a hugely humanitarian softhearted lovely woman, and a pretty cold, calculating lawyer slash judge," said Totenberg said to me on the phone. "It's a hard act to match for almost anybody."

But we really can all become more notorious in our own lives and communities. What it comes down to is finding passion in both the job you do and the people you surround yourself with, working hard and putting your best work forward, and standing up for what's right, every time.

Because no matter how far we've come, there is always further to go.

2

On Equality for All

NATHAN BADER WAS JUST THIRTEEN years old when he arrived on the shores of the United States as a Jewish immigrant from Odessa, Ukraine. He had no money and would ultimately never attend high school. He later became a furrier, "when the last thing a person could afford was a fur coat."[1] He met and married Celia née Amster, and in 1933, the couple gave birth to their second child, Joan Ruth Bader, during the height of the Great Depression.

Sixty years later, that daughter of Jewish immigrants took her place on the bench of the Supreme Court. Deciding to occupy a remote location on the second floor instead of occupying an office near the other justices, Ginsburg set up camp over a series of rooms where she could have her clerks nearby and not be distracted by protestors outside the building.[2] The new justice filled her office with modern art and promptly hung a framed injunction from the Torah that reads, "Justice, Justice shalt thou pursue."[3]

It is from this office where Ginsburg has strategically fought for equality for all—not just women but men too, as well as "African Americans, Hispanics, gays, immigrants, the poor, the disabled," as Jane De Hart writes.[4] Though she is most highly honored for her work in women and the law, RBG has worked toward protecting anyone who is discriminated against or stereotyped within United States law.

"America is known as a country that welcomes people to its shores," she said during an interview with journalist Katie Couric in 2017. "All kinds of people. The image of the Statue of Liberty with Emma Lazarus's famous poem. She lifts her lamp and welcomes people to the golden shore, where they will not experience prejudice because of the color of their skin, the religious faith that they follow."[5]

It is easy to idolize Justice Ginsburg as a pioneer of women's rights but admiring that work alone would ignore not only the passion she has for equal rights for all people, but the effort and work that she has put in to protecting the rights of humans everywhere. And while her dissents about abortion or gender stereotypes make easily shareable Instagram posts, her words surrounding immigrant rights, rights for people of color, and LGBTQ+ rights should also be amplified.

We can learn from this work just as much as we can from her work for women's rights. We've likely all heard the golden rule: "Treat people how you want to be treated." As a Jewish woman and the child of immigrants, Ginsburg understands what it is like to be treated poorly. She frequently tells of a time during her childhood in which her family was driving in Pennsylvania when they passed an inn that had a sign on the lawn reading, "No Dogs or Jews Allowed."[6] It is no surprise that after experiencing prejudice firsthand, RBG dedicated her life to securing equal rights for all. Her life serves as a reminder to speak up when you see any injustice.

Her building-block approach to the law is not quite as apparent through these cases, but it is still there. Ginsburg's fundamental belief that the court should make incremental changes instead of overarching decisions shines through. She also utilizes something she calls comparative side-glances, or looking at foreign courts, in order to learn what has or has not worked for others. This provides an important lesson: learning from others can only strengthen your own work and decisions, both in providing good examples of what worked and showing you what to avoid. Finally, her record is proof that your passions and dedication are not, and maybe should not be, limited to one thing.

★ ★ ★

The justice has had her share of wins and losses when it comes to fighting for others, just as she has fighting for women's equality. She always pushes on, believing that everyone benefits in a more diverse and inclusive society. RBG thinks people should work together toward helping others, all while understanding and celebrating each other's differences.[7]

And though the times have changed—both due to shifts in society and thanks to her tireless dedication to the law—and the country looks very different than it did when Ginsburg was first inspired to be a lawyer, there is still a large challenge ahead.

"That challenge, I believe, is to make and keep our communities places where we can tolerate, even celebrate, our differences, while pulling together for the common good.

'E Pluribus Unum'—of many, one—is the main challenge," Ginsburg once wrote. "It is my hope for our country and world."[8]

RBG started addressing this challenge straight out of Cornell when her husband Marty was sent to Fort Sill, Oklahoma's artillery school. They spent their first two years of marriage in the town, and while Marty attended school, Ruth got a job at a local Social Security office. Soon after, she started to "bend the rules, just a little," explain the authors of *Notorious RBG*.[9] At the time, many Native Americans in the area did not have birth certificates because no official cared enough to make them, so many people coming into the Social Security office were turned away due to lack of valid ID. Ginsburg made the decision that as long as someone looked sixty-five years old, "a hunting or fishing license would do."[10]

She firmly believes that no one should be hampered by "faulty procedure" or "lack of financial resources," wrote author Jane De Hart, who penned a biography of Ginsburg over the course of fifteen years.[11]

The Warren Court, the sixteen-year period when Earl Warren was the Chief Justice, extended the right to counsel to people charged with felonies, required that suspects be advised of their right to remain silent and consult an attorney, as well as addressed other civil rights and liberties and the power of the government.[12] These decisions were eroded over the years, and since Ginsburg supports many of them, she has been left fighting to preserve the remnants.[13]

This idea that the government should not foster inequality has guided Ginsburg's fight. In *Sisters in Law*, lawyer and author Linda Hirsham again credits RBG's Cornell professor Robert Cushman with the justice's judicial philosophy, which is entrenched in the belief that everyone deserves equal access to justice.[14]

This philosophy is perhaps clearest when Ginsburg talks about preserving the right to counsel. She believes that the criminal justice system can only function if defendants all have fair access to court.[15] She has been quoted saying that she is dedicated to the idea that no one should be treated as less-than by the government.[16]

It was a slave owner who wrote the most important statement about equality in the Declaration of Independence, Ginsburg pointed out during an interview with *The New Yorker*.[17] Today, however, Thomas Jefferson would likely agree that the idea of equality will change as society changes, she continued. She said that commercial law expanded, which meant so did the idea of due process. In a similar way, equal protection will continue to grow and evolve.[18]

Law professor Lisa Kern Griffin explains in *The Legacy of Ruth Bader Ginsburg* that Ginsburg cares more about what happens in the court than whatever reason the defendant ended up there.[19] Ginsburg's idea of a fair criminal justice process contains many principles of equality, but is mostly focused on the idea that the government should not be creating inequality and should instead be trying to remedy past injustices.[20]

Essentially, Griffin writes, criminal defendants deserve access to favorable evidence that can help them mount a defense, attorneys necessary to do just that, and a fair jury.[21] Once they receive all three, the defendants' constitutional rights are protected.

The overarching idea held by Ginsburg is that everyone, no matter what crime they have been accused of committing, should have the ability to fight the claims against them while inside the criminal justice process. When people are granted their rights, the system is fair and equal.[22]

★ ★ ★

In June of 1958, Mildred Jeter and Richard Loving, an interracial couple, drove from their home in Virginia to Washington, DC, in order to get married. At the time, Virginia was one of fifteen states that banned interracial marriage, and Jeter was of mixed African American and Native American descent and Loving was white. Five weeks after their wedding, someone tipped off the police, who raided their house in the middle of the night while the couple was in bed, declared their marriage license no good, and sent them to jail. Loving was luckier—he spent the night in jail—but Jeter spent six nights in jail. Later, when they appeared in court, the couple was told they could spend a year in jail or could leave the state and not return for twenty-five years. Ultimately, Loving and Jeter moved to DC, and, with the help of the ACLU, their case made it to the Supreme Court, where a unanimous decision declared the marriage ban violated the Equal Protections Clause of the Constitution.[23]

Ginsburg frequently references this case, *Loving v. Virginia*, which she has said is one of the most important cases ever decided by the US Supreme Court.[24] She feels like it shows how far the country has come in legal equality and gives her hope for the future. During a speech at the Federal Judicial High School Teachers Program in 2009, Ginsburg said that she, like Mildred Loving, was able to see grand changes throughout her life. When Ginsburg and Justice

Sandra Day O'Connor graduated from law school, no one would hire them because of their gender. In the 1950s, it was impossible to believe two women would be sitting on the Supreme Court, just like it was impossible to believe the president of the United States would someday be an African American man born to an interracial couple. RBG said that though there is of course a long way to go in order to make sure everyone in the United States can enjoy equal protection of the law, it is worth being optimistic when you look at how far we have come as a country.[25]

This determination and hope might be what has propelled Ginsburg to historically support affirmative action. Author De Hart writes that Ginsburg understands that both structural and cultural factors contribute to discrimination, which helped her craft creative proposals to address affirmative action during the late 1970s. De Hart also says the justice refuses to hide the disdain she holds for those who attempt to block equal rights for all.[26]

In 1967, Ginsburg, at the time a professor at Rutgers, adamantly supported a proposal to establish a Minority Student Program at the then majority-white, majority-male Rutgers Law School. The program was accepted and had a great impact on the student body, and helped it become more "racially and gender diverse."[27] The program went on to help diversify the bar in New Jersey and across the country.

In 2009 while giving a speech titled "Remarks on the Value of Diversity" at the Insitut d'Etudes Politiques, Ginsburg said that many modern constitutions either allow or require affirmative action in order to battle decades of inequality and to help people who are disadvantaged or oppressed based purely on the population they were born into. The justice went on to mention India's 1950 constitution, which had multiple affirmative action provisions but clearly stated the government should help promote the educational and economic needs of the "weaker sections of people."[28]

In 2013, Ginsburg was the only justice who dissented in *Fisher v. University of Texas,* a case that doubted the legality of the university's affirmative action program. The program guaranteed Texas high school seniors in the top 10 percent of their class automatic admission to the University of Texas. At the University of Texas, three-quarters of the freshman class was admitted under that program, and the remaining members were evaluated on varying factors, such as leadership qualities, family life, skills, and race. Abigail Fisher was a white student who was not in the top 10 percent of her class. She sued the university for race discrimination after she was rejected from the school.[29] Both the District Court and the Fifth Circuit Court of Appeals ruled in favor of the university. But the Supreme Court sent the case back to the Fifth Circuit and told them to make sure there was a "necessary" reason for the UT program.[30] Ginsburg dissented, saying she would have affirmed the judgment of the court of appeals.[31] Years later, Ginsburg was in the majority opinion when the Supreme Court upheld the program at UT.[32]

That same year, Ginsburg read a scathing dissent when the Supreme Court ruled 5–4 to strike down a provision of the US 1965 Voting Rights Act in which states had to get approval or "preclearance" from the Justice Department before enacting big changes to voting laws in any given state. In her dissent, she famously wrote, "Throwing out preclearance when it has worked and is continuing to work to stop discriminatory changes is like throwing away your umbrella in a rainstorm because you are not getting wet."[33]

However, it would be an oversight to not mention a pertinent criticism that has been leveled against Ginsburg: though she is committed to racial justice and has led efforts to fix the effects of race discrimination, she has only hired one African American law clerk in her twenty-five years on the Supreme Court.[34] She never had any black clerks during her thirteen years on the US Court of Appeals for the District of Columbia Circuit.[35] And according to the *Washington Post,* when accounting the hiring of all racial minorities since 2005, only "12 percent of Ginsburg's clerks were nonwhite."[36]

Paul Butler, a professor in law at Georgetown University, who wrote that *Washington Post* article, concludes it by saying that there is no doubt Ginsburg forcefully pushes "back on retrenchments on racial justice," but that while he hopes "Ginsburg serves for 10 more years," he also hopes that "each of those years she hires clerks of color to remedy a substantial blemish on an otherwise remarkable career."[37]

These facts provide an important lesson: there is always room for improvement, even within a career as impeccable as Ginsburg's. No one can ever be fully perfect (and who would want that anyway?), and all we can do is try to continue learning about each other and our different experiences. We have to do our best to listen to those who speak up, ask questions, acknowledge our mistakes, make adjustments, and remain intentional about the way we conduct ourselves and the work we are doing.

★ ★ ★

Justice Ginsburg's view of the world is informed through the federal court system, and her understanding of the law informs her ability to fight for equality. Obviously, not all of us view the world through the court system, but we can all learn from how she looks at the past to try and to correct for the future. We can also learn from her use of comparative side-glances, or looking at rulings made in national, multinational, or international courts other than the Supreme Court.

For example, if you work in Hollywood or the film industry, you can acknowledge those who have been under-represented in movies throughout history and try to correct that gap. If you are a salesperson, you can learn the ways that different people have tried to sell a similar product and see what worked and what didn't. As a journalist, I can check in with myself to make sure that the story I am working on has not already been told, and also to make sure that I am the right person to be writing that particular story.

Former clerk Paul Schiff Berman wrote in *The Legacy of Ruth Bader Ginsburg* that RBG is an advocate of seeking wisdom from international sources. In an ideal world, state courts would respect each other's authorities and judgments, and many of her decisions aim to make that world a reality.[38]

Take the Supreme Court's 1954 *Brown v. Board of Education* decision, which was reported around the world. Ginsburg once wrote that this decision helped push for further changes in law and in practice that emphasized equality and dignity for all the world's people.[39] Comparative side-glances go both ways: other countries can utilize and listen to decisions made by US courts as well.[40]

While working as the associate director of Columbia Law School, Ginsburg spent time in Sweden and even taught herself the language. During this period, she learned a lot about how women's equality in Sweden was very different than that of the United States.

There was a woman named Eva Moberg in Sweden who wrote a column in the paper *Stockholm Daily*. The headline was "Why should the woman have two jobs and the man only one?" and the basic idea of the piece was that women were expected to go to work every day and then come home and maintain the home. Women were meant to have paying jobs, get dinner on the table for their family every night, make sure the children had all the clothes they need and that they went to the doctor while the man of the house was expected to take out the garbage. The idea that he should do more than that was very interesting to Ginsburg and raised a lot of questions for her.[41]

While in Sweden, Ginsburg came to understand that what works for citizens of the United States might not work for others. However, there was something to learn from foreign systems as the United States attempted to figure out what was best.[42] It comes down to this: many believe that United States' experiences and decisions can help other countries create their own constitutions and judicial systems. So why can't the United States learn from others who are attempting to build governmental branches or secure basic rights for their people?[43]

The takeaway: seeing how others deal with similar problems can give you—or in Ginsburg's case, the court—another perspective of what could work (or can't work) and what is acceptable in society. If you are faced with a dilemma, it will help to look and see how other people have handled it. Your plan forward may be validated by what you find, or you may see something that scares you off and forces you to find a better solution. Say you're a teacher, and the course material isn't clicking with a particular student. You can look and see what other teachers around the world have tried and said was successful. You can then try those methods with your student. It is a similar idea to when you are planning a trip—you ask friends or relatives who have already been to that place what you should see and get advice on what to avoid.

Ginsburg agrees with former Justice O'Connor when it comes to comparative side-glances. O'Connor once said that other legal systems were always innovating, experimenting, and searching for new solutions to new legal problems that seemed to pop up every day. There was no reason why the US Supreme Court could not learn and benefit from their efforts.[44]

Though comparative side-glances have faced criticism by some, they are not all that new to the Supreme Court. A study cowritten by Steven Calabresi, a Northwestern University law professor and cofounder of the Federalist Society, a network of conservative lawyers, wrote that "foreign law is cited in concurring and dissenting opinions joined by six of the nine justices in *Dred Scott v. Sandford* and in the Court's opinion in the anti-polygamy case, *Reynolds v. United States.*"[45]

In no way does Ginsburg think that looking at how another country does something means that the United States must do it that way too—just like how you don't always take every piece of advice you hear from friends or family on any one topic. Oftentimes it's the exact opposite. Comparing how things are done elsewhere might help us decide what to do, but also might show us what we should avoid.[46] American judges can already consult any material they would like while making a decision, so why not look abroad for both inspiration or for examples of what hasn't worked? The Constitutional Court of South Africa, the German Constitutional Court, or the European Court of Human Rights might hold the answers to a question the United States courts are pondering.[47]

Courts frequently look at past decisions and stored knowledge in order to make decisions. These side-glances can build upon that collective understanding of what solutions may or may not work. Ginsburg hopes that we all approach foreign legal matters with a sensitive understanding of our differences and individual imperfections, but those differences should not stop us from accepting wisdom that those countries may have about a matter the United States is facing.[48]

The overarching lesson from comparative side-glances is an easy one: there is always more to learn, and it is okay to embrace what others have done. Just as judges may learn from the experimentations of others, as Berman writes in *The Legacy of Ruth Bader Ginsburg*,[49] we can all learn by seeing what has worked (and hasn't worked) for others. Recognize differences but acknowledge that we can all learn from each other.

"I think she's very much an internationalist in that way too, she is interested in how other countries approach the same kinds of legal problems America faces and she's not afraid to look beyond what our own history tells us and instead embrace what other countries have gone through because they might have something to teach us, even about ourselves," Dodson told me during our interview.

★ ★ ★

Nina Totenberg once wrote that Ginsburg frequently stands up for things she feels strongly about through her actions, not just her words.[50]

For example, the work Ginsburg did on sex-based discrimination helped preserve some legal protections for LGBTQ+ people. As an article published in *them* explains, the words "sex" and "gender" are basically interchangeable when it comes to the law as it applies to sex-based discrimination.[51] Laws that prevent discrimination on the basis of sex have frequently (though not always) been interpreted to include protections for transgender and queer people, writer and editor Naveen Kumar explains in the article. By launching the fight for women's equality, Ginsburg "was perhaps inadvertently launching the fight against anti-LGBTQ+ discrimination as well." Kumar writes, "Just as getting fired because you're a woman is unlawful, the argument goes, so should getting fired for being transgender, gay, lesbian, or bisexual—all of which are aspects of identity necessarily tied to one's sex."[52]

An article published in *ThinkProgress* elaborated on this idea as well. Journalist Zack Ford says the legal fight portrayed in *On the Basis of Sex* is still relevant for the LGBTQ+ community today. He asserts that LGTBTQ+ people have also argued they should be "protected under the umbrella of legal precedents that Ginsburg helped set."[53]

Just as Ginsburg can be seen doing in the movie *On the Basis of Sex,* Ford writes, "LGBTQ people have argued that laws that treat them differently violate their due process and equal protection rights." He continues, "these contentions allowed same-sex couples to prevail in 2015, when the Supreme Court enshrined their right to marry."[54]

Ginsburg also strongly believes that everyone should be free to marry whomever they'd like. In 2013, she joined a major Supreme Court decision that the federal government must recognize gay marriages (the court had also declared California's ban on same-sex marriages unconstitutional). That year she became the first sitting Supreme Court justice to preside at a same-sex wedding ceremony when she officiated the wedding of Michael Kaiser, the president of the John F. Kennedy Center for the Performing Arts in Washington, and John Roberts, an economist, in 2013.[55]

Then, in 2015, the justice voted in favor of granting same-sex couples the right to get married in all fifty states, successfully allowing marriage equality in America.

The 5–4 ruling in the landmark decision made history. When the Supreme Court was hearing arguments for the case, Ginsburg was outspoken about the concept of marriage. During the hearing, she talked about how marriage today has changed and evolved from ideas of marriage in the past.

"[The old conception of marriage] was a relationship of a dominant male to a subordinate female that ended as a result of this court's decision in 1982 when Louisiana's Head and Master Rule was struck down," she said, according to an article by *The Independent*. "Would that be a choice that state should [still] be allowed to have? To cling to marriage the way it once was?"[56]

Since this first wedding, Ginsburg has presided over multiple LGBT marriages.[57]

When asked what it means for a Supreme Court justice to preside over a same-sex marriage, Ginsburg responded, "I think it will be one more statement that people who love each other and want to live together should be able to enjoy the blessings and the strife in the marriage relationship."[58]

In Ginsburg's eyes, progress was made during the LGBT movement when more people started coming out as gay and lesbian, forcing their neighbors, communities, and friends to acknowledge that they knew, respected, and cared for someone who was gay or lesbian.[59]

Ginsburg's goal when it comes to the law is to "get it right" and "keep it tight."[60] As shown through her steady takedown of laws that discriminated against women, Ginsburg prefers narrow rules, and generally avoids grand pronouncements. She has been called a "lawyer's lawyer" or a "judge's judge," according to multiple sources, for this way of approaching the law. She is patient, employing a method where individual cases that build on each other sometimes come to the court many years apart.[61]

"I think she understands that the court has neither money nor an army, so it can't enforce its own decisions. It has to rely on the other political branches to enforce its decisions, and it has to rely on the legitimacy that it gets from the public in order to get those political branches to follow the court," Scott Dodson said to me during a phone interview.

Dodson said that Ginsburg, like many of the justices, understands that the court cannot make many strong pronouncements, especially not on a regular basis. Therefore, while Ginsburg's approach is due to her own beliefs, it is also a part of the function of the court.

"[The court] has to move more incrementally if it's going to retain its own legitimacy," Dodson said.

Ginsburg does not want courts to get ahead of democratic sentiment and has in fact warned them against doing so.[62] In her mind, it is not the court's job to find problems or laws to fix. Instead, judges should be communicating with the other political branches in order to stay abreast of society's wants and needs.[63]

★ ★ ★

I could go on and on about the other inequalities that Ginsburg fights against, but the point is clear. Though her pursuits for equality under the law cover a broad range of subjects, Ginsburg's method of addressing the inequalities is always the same: instead of broad, sweeping laws, she prefers to stick to a slow, methodical process that uses persuasion over anger. As lawyer and author Linda Hirshman puts it, Ginsburg exhibits her strengths through her knowledge of civil procedure and understanding of constitutional doctrine.[64]

What can those of us who do not sit on the Supreme Court take away from this approach?

The first lesson is one we've been through already in Chapter 1, but it is so integral to Ruth Bader Ginsburg's life that it is worth repeating: focus on what matters by utilizing a plan that takes small, incremental (but instrumental) steps toward your goal.

Dodson told me about a second lesson that echoes the first: know what you want (even if you want multiple things) and don't be afraid to be dedicated enough to actually get it.

"I think also her dedication is really a virtue; she was dedicated in so many ways, she was dedicated to ideas, she was dedicated to whatever job she held at the time, she was dedicated to Marty, and so being able to understand what you really want out of life and go get it and do what it takes to go get it, I think is a tremendously important message for young people out there," Dodson said.

And finally: never give up hope.

"I think she sees the country as moving in a progressive way even if at times it's two steps forward one step back or sometimes the opposite, one step forward two steps back, but in the long run, I think she thinks there is great room for hope and the country will move in the direction she thinks it should," said Dodson.

PART II

The Importance of Relationships

"And I betray no secret in reporting that, without him, I would not have gained a seat on the Supreme Court."
> —*Ruth Bader Ginsburg on her husband in an op-ed she wrote for the* New York Times, *published in 2016*[1]

★ ★ ★

"Collegiality is crucial to the success of our mission. We could not do the job the Constitution assigns to us if we didn't—to use one of Justice Antonin Scalia's favorite expressions: 'Get over it.'"
> —*Ruth Bader Ginsburg on the relationships with other members of the Supreme Court*[2]

3

On Marrying Somebody Like Marty

IT WAS SUPPOSED TO BE a blind date, but Marty Ginsburg cheated. He saw Ruth Bader on Cornell's campus and convinced his friend to arrange the meeting because he thought she was cute. The two were both seeing other people (Marty had a girlfriend at Smith College, while Ruth had maintained a relationship with a boy she had met at summer camp who attended Columbia University), so the date was only meant to introduce the two as "safe" company for each other.[1] But the two soon realized they shared an intense connection, intellectually and emotionally.[2] As Ruth always says, Marty was the first boy who cared that she had a brain.[3]

As for Marty, he realized the extent of her intelligence on their second date. It was then that he understood she was not only really smart, but she wasn't "glib," Marty once said of his wife. He once told the authors of *My Own Words* that more than anyone else he'd ever met, Ruth is not afraid of "dead air time." If you ask her something, she will stop and think through her answer before responding. At the time, he said that she had done this for the more than five decades he has known her, and still did it at dinner.[4]

Their love story proceeded quickly and soon became legendary. Marty said he knew that he wanted to spend his life with Ruth before[5] she decided the same, but he said it was clear to him early on that he was going to have a happier life if she was in it.[6] They became a couple her junior year (he was a year older than she) and were inseparable.[7]

His marriage proposal, asked while they were in the car, elicited a loud yes from Ruth. They were married in 1954, in the backyard of Marty's parents' Long Island home.[8] After the ceremony, Ruth's new mother-in-law took her aside to tell her, "In every good marriage, it pays sometimes to be a little deaf." At the same time, she handed Ruth wax earplugs.[9] To this day, Ruth says she used that advice in both her marriage and on the court.[10]

In a world of dating apps and crowded bars, of rom-coms and high expectations, it can sometimes be hard to imagine a partnership like that found between Ruth Bader and Marty Ginsburg. But it is an important reminder to all of us that this level of intimacy and support can exist in a relationship. Your idea of a family might not look like RBG's. Maybe you don't believe in marriage, maybe you have more than one life partner, or maybe you see yourself building a family in a non-traditional way. No matter what your definition of a partner is, I still think the lesson is still there: Find yourself a partner like Marty. Someone who empowers and uplifts you, who makes you laugh, and who not only sees your career goals as being as important as theirs but goes above and beyond to help you achieve them.

★ ★ ★

In order to truly understand how special their relationship was, we need to acknowledge how rare a marriage like theirs was at the time. It is well-documented that their partnership was built on "mutual respect and equality—and a willingness to share domestic duties."[11]

Ginsburg knows that she had the great fortune of sharing her life with a partner who was "truly extraordinary for his generation." At only eighteen, Marty already believed that a woman's work, whether at home or at a job, was just as important as a man's work. "I attended law school in days when women were not wanted by most members of the legal profession. I became a lawyer because Marty and his parents supported that choice unreservedly," she said.[12]

Ruth later said that the best decision she made was marrying Marty.[13] The couple celebrated fifty-six years of marriage before Marty's death in 2010, and not only did Marty Ginsburg support his wife's endeavors in the law, but he actively fought for her to get higher positions, more prestige, and more power.

"It certainly wasn't the norm," said Jane De Hart, author of *Ruth Bader Ginsburg: A Life,* a 540-page book about the justice's life. "I asked her about that, and I also asked a couple of her friends about that, and the consensus was . . . that he was obviously very much so in love with her and was content to do whatever it took to make the marriage succeed."

When they were married, Marty had just finished his first year at Harvard Law School. Now that she had graduated from Cornell, Ruth was going to join him. She had long ago decided that whatever career they chose, they would choose it together.

"I think that meeting Marty and falling in love with him at such a young time in her life and needy time in her life was really just dumb luck," NPR's Nina Totenberg told me. She has known Ruth Ginsburg for nearly fifty years. "And the person she is, is at least in part formed by that marriage . . . I don't think she could've done what she's done without Marty and she certainly wouldn't be on the Supreme Court."

Before they could go to law school, they had to spend two years stationed at Fort Sill, which gave them a two-year respite from the outside world. Ruth got pregnant with their first child in 1955, before the couple was supposed to go back to school, which worried Ruth, as she would be the mother of a young child and a student.[14] But Marty's family had become her family, and her father-in-law took his turn giving her advice.

"Ruth, if you don't want to go to law school, you have the best reason in the world; no one will think less of you," he said to her. "But if you really want to go to law school, you will stop feeling sorry for yourself and you will find a way to do it."[15]

And she did find a way, with Marty's help. When she made the *Harvard Law Review*, Marty took care of Jane for two weeks at his parents' house in the summer so Ruth could head back to school early. During the school year, baby Jane could be found crawling around the *Law Review* office. After graduation, when Ruth went to Sweden to study civil procedure, Marty took care of Jane, who was enrolled in private school, for the first six weeks (with the help of a housekeeper). Jane then joined Ruth abroad.[16] A decade after they had their daughter, the couple had a son, James. As time went on, Marty went on to have his own very successful and lucrative career as a high-powered tax attorney before becoming a professor at New York University, Columbia, and, later, Georgetown.[17]

Like all relationships, Ruth and Marty's hit roadblocks, but the two faced more than their fair share. For one, Marty, like Ruth, suffered from multiple bouts of cancer, the first when he was a third-year student at Harvard Law and Ruth was a second-year student. Their daughter Jane was only three. He was diagnosed with testicular cancer, which had spread to four lymph nodes. Doctors told the couple that the chances of his survival were "almost nil."[18] He had two surgeries and daily radiation therapy, leaving him weakened and sick.

"When he was sick, you couldn't have had a sweeter and better caregiver than she was," said former Stanford Law professor Barbara Babcock. "She was giving up a lot of herself and all of her free time to take care of him, and she didn't complain. She was wonderful."

Ruth took control of both their lives and studies, ordering Marty's classmates to take notes on carbon paper, which she then copied. She typed up all his papers, on top of her own classwork, while taking care of Jane and running the *Harvard Law Review*. This is when her infamous work hours began—she functioned on very little sleep as she stayed up through the night to finish her work after she had helped Marty with his and put Jane to bed.

Of that time in her life, Ginsburg said that they took each day at a time and lived it the best they could. She also grew confident in her juggling capabilities that semester.[19]

And juggle she did. In fact, Ruth has said that having a daughter gave her a "better sense of what life is."[20] She attributes a lot of her success in law school to her daughter.

"I went to class about 8:30 and I came home at four o'clock, that was children's hour. It was a total break in my day, and children's hour continued until Jane went to sleep," Ruth has explained. Afterward, she was happy to go back to her studying. "I felt each part of my life gave me respite from the other."[21]

When the tables turned, and Ruth got colon cancer in 1999 and then pancreatic cancer in 2009, Marty was at her side.[22]

But even more than being there in sickness, the two were there together in health. There is no question in anyone's mind, including Ruth's, that she would not have her seat on the Supreme Court bench if it weren't for Marty.

★ ★ ★

It was Marty, in fact, who brought Ruth her first gender discrimination case. Marty was reading a tax case about a single man taking care of his mom. The man didn't qualify for a tax break that a single woman taking care of a parent would qualify for. Marty went into Ruth's office and handed her the case; she quickly responded that she didn't read tax briefs. Marty pushed her to read this one. She went back into Marty's office five minutes later to declare they were taking the case.[23] This case shifted Ruth's career from an academic professor to a successful and fireball advocate, which later contributed to her next career on the highest bench in the land.[24]

We all know what happens next—Ruth becomes a rock star litigator and successfully takes five cases that challenge gender bias and discrimination in the law to the Supreme Court. She starts the Women's Rights Project at the ACLU. She usually looks for Marty in a room when she speaks in public.[25] While RBG is always very clear that she does not do any of this alone, and thanks the many women and men who helped her during this time, the next step, landing her positions as a judge and then a justice, a lot of that credit has to go to Marty.

Ruth Ginsburg is not a transactional person, and she "never asked for anything in her life," explained Dahlia Lithwick, a lawyer and reporter who writes about law and politics. RBG got her seat at the court because Marty lobbied for her. Even before that, however, he lobbied for her to get a seat on the US Court of Appeals for the District of Columbia Circuit Court.

Babcock, another pioneer of women's equality in the law and who, like Ruth, taught classes about women and law but at Stanford University, told me about the time Marty called her to ask if she would "lend a supportive hand" in the effort to secure Ruth her confirmations on both the DC Circuit and the Supreme Court. Babcock and Marty knew each other through Ruth and through other friends who were tax lawyers.

"[Marty] has always thought, and you know he knows her well, that [Ruth] would be a great justice, that she was so extremely fair and thoughtful about everything she did, and he just always pushed it," Babcock said. "I'm not sure he even said 'can you help,' he said 'when will you start helping.'"

Babcock did help, because even though Ruth never would have called on her in that way, they were playing for the same team, and fighting the same fight.

"That's so brave in our world, in our lawyers' world, that's just a very brave and loving thing to do, I was knocked out by it," said Babcock of Marty helping Ruth.

This was just one of many times that Marty went to bat for his wife. Ruth told the *Washington Post* in 2013 that Marty "became my campaign manager"[26] when she was trying to garner support to get nominated by President Bill Clinton to serve on the Supreme Court. Since Clinton was worried that the "women were against" RBG, Marty made sure to find powerful women to write letters of support for the DC judge.[27] The *Post* also wrote that Marty "organized a letter-writing campaign so aggressive it earned press attention."[28] Ruth has famously repeated, "I betray no secret in reporting that, without him, I would not have gained a seat on the US Supreme Court."[29] Even then–Associate White House Counsel Ron Klain said of Ruth's 1993 nomination that even though she should have been picked no matter what based on her qualifications, she would not have gotten the nomination for the Supreme Court if her husband had not done every possible thing he could think of to make it happen.[30]

Robert A. Katzmann, now Chief Judge of the United States Court of Appeals for the Second Circuit, wrote about Ruth's path to the court in *The Legacy of Ruth Bader Ginsburg*. After RBG was nominated, Katzmann got a call from Senator Daniel Patrick Moynihan, her Senate sponsor, asking if

Katzmann would be special counsel pro bono to him and then–Judge Ginsburg. Katzmann claims he said yes before Senator Moynihan had even fully voiced the question.[31]

He spent that summer with RBG as she made the rounds on the Hill. But Katzmann also writes that at least once a day he checked in with her husband. Marty had the ability not only to look at the big picture, but also to pay attention to detail, and his judgment was worth following.[32] Katzmann treasured these conversations, which frequently included laughing about some very funny, but also perceptive, comment that Marty had made.[33]

"I think it's impossible to understand her career and her success without understanding it as a result of a partnership," said Joan Williams, a professor of law at UC Hasting and an expert in women and the law. "I mean, she never would've become a Supreme Court justice without him. He did all the politicking, all the glad-handing, that there's just no way in God's green Earth that she would've been so successful."

Once Ruth did get on the court, Marty was right there, taking care of his wife and being her biggest cheerleader. Totenberg said that Marty used to call Ruth and tell her it was time to come home. The justice would hang up and keep working, and Marty would call back an hour later and say, "It's Marty, it really is time to come home." And then eventually, Marty would just go gather his wife from her chambers. He made sure she ate a meal a day and slept, sometimes.[34]

When I get really busy with work, I sometimes forget to eat breakfast or lunch. My current roommate thinks that this is absurd. But it makes it all the clearer to me that Ruth Bader Ginsburg was able to start keeping this inhuman schedule because Marty was there to balance things out. That is not to say you need to get married or have a partner in order to be successful or make your dreams come true, that's not it at all, but instead is a reminder to surround yourself with people who are willing to help you thrive through gestures both big and small. Whether it is a friend or a partner or a sibling, we all need to have people there to remind us to sleep, shower, and eat.

★ ★ ★

And RBG ate well, because Marty was a great cook—he even baked his own bread, which the French Ambassador once called "the best baguettes outside of France"[35]—while Ruth was not. When they were first married, Ruth was in charge of making the weekday meals, while Marty was in charge of weekend and guest meals. Ruth had seven meals she could make, and when they got to the seventh meal, she started over again.[36] Though their daughter Jane claims to have not seen a vegetable until she was fourteen years old, Ruth was eventually booted out of the kitchen by her children.[37]

In fact, according to *Notorious RBG*, a young Jane once described their family by saying that her mother was the one doing all the thinking, while her dad was the one doing all the cooking.[38] After Marty's death, a cookbook was made in his honor by the spouses of the other Supreme Court judges. It is called *The Chef Supreme*.[39] Be warned, his recipe for that best baguette is over fifty steps long.[40]

Marty's love of cooking even inspired his nephew. Daniel Stiepleman, who ultimately made the movie *On the Basis of Sex* about the only court case Marty and Ruth ever worked on together, remembers Marty's cooking from holiday parties during his childhood. Stiepleman tells *The New Yorker* that at one of those parties, a grown-up asked him what he wanted to be when he grew up.

"I said, 'I want to be like Uncle Martin,' and the person said, 'Oh, you want to be a lawyer?' And I said, 'No, I'm going to be a cooking dad!'"[41]

Ruth and Marty lovingly raised their children, taking them to art and culture events (like the opera), sending them to summer camp, and going on vacation together to places like St. Thomas in the Virgin Islands. The children may not have always appreciated their mother's "tenacity on matters of posture, tidiness, or diet,"[42] but for the most part, the family made their juggling act work. And this love and humor continued on to their children's offspring—like any good grandfather, Marty once had two of his grandchildren convinced that the statue on top of the Capitol building in Washington, DC, was him.[43]

★ ★ ★

Though much credit is given to Marty for "sacrificing" parts of his life, it's necessary to also recognize that the support went both ways.

"When Marty was starting out in law practice and eager to make partner, I was responsible for the lion's share of taking care of Jane and the home, but that balance changed when the women's movement came alive and Marty appreciated the importance of the work I was doing, so then I became the person whose career came first," Ginsburg once said.[44]

De Hart emphasized to me that there was a time when Ruth's career took a back seat to Marty's.

"You have to remember that his career took precedence in the early years, she bore more than her share in parenting and it was really, I mean she was in her early forties when she was doing the ACLU litigation, and at that point he was determined to do as much as he could, consistent with the demands of his own very successful career," De Hart said.

Ruth herself told Katie Couric during an interview in 2014 that devoted life partners take care of and help each other when needed. Marty thought Ruth's work was as important as his, and that made a huge difference in Ruth's life.[45] They were truly equals, and in turn, their careers were of equal importance.

For Valentine's Day 2019, their son, James Ginsburg, wrote about his mom and dad's love story for *The Hollywood Reporter*. James explains once Marty made partner at his firm, he emphasized the importance of family, making sure the workers in his department were headed home by 7 p.m. to have dinner with their "loved ones."[46] This is something Ruth did later on in her own career—multiple clerks told me that she has always been incredibly understanding of their coming and goings based on the needs of their family (as long as the work got done, of course).

When Ruth got her "good job" in DC, as Marty called it, many people were stunned by the idea that a man as successful as Marty would give up his law practice and a tenured position at Columbia Law School in order to follow his wife. But according to James, Ruth had followed him to New York, and it was Marty's turn to follow her.[47] Besides, Marty excelled at being the spouse of a justice—he always made Ruth's clerks a cake for their birthday, and he would find time to read quietly in Ruth's chambers while she worked.

We should let Marty speak for himself. He told the *New York Times* in 1993, "I have been supportive of my wife since the beginning of time, and she has been supportive of me. It's not sacrifice; it's family."[48]

★ ★ ★

The age-old idea that opposites attract really seemed to be at play with Ruth and Marty.

"He was gigantic, she's tiny; he was loud, she's stark; he's gregarious, she's shy; he's a cook, she's a terrible cook," said David Post, who twice clerked for Ginsburg. But they really fed off each other, he continued. "Both parties thought the world of each other. It was really quite something."

Former clerk Heather Elliott told me during our interview to look up a story that she had previously submitted for a reunion and is now documented in the book *The Notorious RBG*.[49] The story goes like this. Late one night, Ruth was working while Marty was reading, and Elliot had to talk to the justice about research she was doing. While Elliot was talking, Marty got off the couch and walked toward her. Elliott was worried she had said something dumb and was confused as to why Marty would come over. Marty gently fixed RBG's collar, which had somehow become rumpled, and then went back to his book. Elliott writes that she will never forget the "comfortable intimacy" she witnessed in that moment.[50]

This is not to say, of course, that the couple didn't face trouble as working parents. There was the time when they were both in school and their daughter Jane stuffed her mouth full of mothballs and had to get her stomach pumped.[51] Or one time when Ruth was in the middle of a lecture at New York University (she had been asked to teach a course in comparative law there on top of her Rutgers schedule), she was passed a note that read, "Son ingested Drano; taken to nearest hospital."[52] RBG rushed to the hospital, where her son had blisters surrounding his mouth and deep burns on his face.[53] Luckily, James had not ingested any of the Drano and was fine, but Jane Ginsburg told Jane De Hart that her mom has yet to forgive herself.[54]

When I saw her speak in December 2018, Ginsburg told the now-famous story of how her son used to get in a lot of trouble and therefore Ruth was receiving a lot of calls from school asking her to come in and handle the situation. One time, James hijacked an elevator and Ruth didn't have time to deal with it. She told the school, "This child has two parents. Please alternate calls." But the calls slowed down, as the school did not want to interrupt Marty (though that might also have to do with the fact Marty responded to the elevator issue with, "Well, how far could he have taken it?").[55]

Clearly, the couple made it through and out the other side, all the while adoring each other. Marty himself frequently told an illustrative story about his fifty-six-year-long marriage to Ruth. They were in New York City to see a play, *Proof.* It was December 2000, just after *Bush v. Gore.* The two were walking down the aisle to their seats following the first-act intermission, and suddenly, it seemed like the whole audience stood up and was applauding. Ruth grinned largely, and so did Marty, who leaned over and whispered loudly to his wife, "I bet you didn't know there's a convention of tax lawyers in town." Ruth, without changing her smile, smacked her husband (not too hard of course), right in the stomach.

"And I give you this picture because it fairly captures our nearly fifty-year happy marriage," Marty has said when telling this story, "during which I have offered up an astonishing number of foolish pronouncements with absolute assurance, and Ruth, with only limited rancor, has ignored almost every one."[56]

★ ★ ★

As shown through their history together, the couple's support for and generosity to each other was seemingly bottomless. The lesson here is that if you choose to have a career and choose to spend your life with someone, it is vital to make sure that person thinks your career is just as important as theirs. If you do want a serious partner, find someone who will pull their weight in terms of whatever family life you decide to have. Find someone who doesn't see changing their life to accommodate you as a sacrifice—and make sure you feel the same way. Find someone who will care for you at your weakest moment, and who will not only push for you to believe in yourself but will push others to believe in you too. (These ideas go for your lifelong friendships and non-romantic partnerships as well: fill your life with people who validate and uplift you both professionally and personally.)

"At public events, he was able to bring her out of her shell a bit, because he was very gregarious, very funny, very talkative, very lively, and she of course is much more quiet and does not put herself out there in quite the same way, and so I think he was good at connecting her to the world in general," said Ruth's former clerk Paul Schiff Berman. "It was wonderful to see how much he enjoyed her and how much she enjoyed him."

Post made another good point. Find a partner who revels in your success. He explained that Marty "thought it was just the coolest thing" that Ruth was becoming an icon (though sadly he did not live to see the extent of T-shirts and tattoos adorned with her face).

"He was just having a very good time of things, he was delighted," Post said, before explaining the idea that some men would be made uncomfortable by their wives' success was the funniest thing to Marty. "That was part of the magic of what they had, he really reveled in her glory."

One lesson that I also think is important to take away from their relationship is that it is okay to ask for help. Again and again I was told that RBG was not the type of person who asked a favor of anyone or bragged about herself, and that Marty is a huge reason she got on the Supreme Court, because he knew she would be great and called in favors to help her get there. But I have also been told that RBG goes above and beyond in helping others—and it's clear that she and Marty both made sacrifices for each other. Though it is important to not exploit the kindness of your loved ones, it is okay to ask them for help in furthering your goals or in times of need. It does not make you any less deserving of the goal for which you are striving.

Another point their relationship highlights: find someone who will make you laugh, no matter how serious you usually are.

"[Justice] Scalia and Marty were two people who really understood making her laugh was a huge currency because she was so reserved and they both just cracked her up and she valued that," said Lithwick.

When I reported on the talk between Ruth Ginsburg and Totenberg in December of 2018, the movie her nephew wrote, *On the Basis of Sex*, had just been released. Totenberg asked the justice what she thought of the marital sex scene between the actors playing Ruth (Felicity Jones) and Marty (Armie Hammer).

"What I thought of it is that Marty would have loved it," the justice remarked with a laugh.[57]

The lightheartedness went both ways. In a *New Yorker* article, author Jeffrey Toobin talks about a time where Justice Ginsburg held a reunion of her law clerks at the Supreme Court. While everyone was mingling, Marty walked over to his wife and put his arm around her. Unbeknownst to the justice, her husband had taped a paper sign to her back that read: "Her Highness."[58]

Finally, find someone who makes you believe in yourself. Ginsburg has said that the "principal advice" she received from her husband throughout their life together was that he made her feel like she was better than she thought she was. She claims to have started out being very unsure and would question herself while writing a brief or preparing an oral argument. But now she sits on the highest court in the land, and when she looks around she says to herself, "It's a hard job, but I can do it at least as well as these guys."[59]

★ ★ ★

After Marty began to have severe back pain, the doctors identified a tumor growing near his spine. They said there was nothing more to be done.[60] When Ruth went to bring her husband home from the hospital, she found a note Marty had written on a yellow pad.[61] She read the letter in full to Nina Totenberg during an interview six years after he died, aired on the podcast *What It Takes*.

"My dearest Ruth," the letter begins. "You are the only person I have loved in my life, setting aside, a bit, parents and kids and their kids, and I have admired and loved you almost since the day we first met at Cornell some 56 years ago."

Ruth paused here to correct her husband, saying that though they had been married fifty-six years, they had actually met about sixty years ago. She then continued reading. Marty wrote that it had been a "treat" to watch his wife make it to the very top of the legal world. He believed he would be in the hospital until Friday, June 25. Before then, he was going to spend time thinking and decide whether to keep fighting or to not, based on the quality of life ahead of him. And though he hoped she would support his final decision, he understood that she may not.

"I will not love you a jot less," he concluded. The letter was signed simply with "Marty."[62]

Totenberg writes that at the time, she had known Ruth Bader Ginsburg for nearly forty years, and that was the first time she had seen her cry.[63]

Marty died on June 27, 2010, soon after the two celebrated their fifty-sixth wedding anniversary.

Ruth Bader Ginsburg was back on the Supreme Court bench the next day, because he would have wanted her there.

"When we were talking about [Marty's] role in helping her become a Supreme Court justice, she mentioned, 'Well, he wanted me to have that after he was gone,'" said Jane De Hart during our interview. "But when she showed up the next day, after his death at court, she said she was there because that's what Marty would've wanted."

Maybe that's the biggest lesson of their relationship: through it all—the kids, the jobs, the cancers, the deaths, the moves, the hard times—they were truly, deeply in love, and they built a life around their passion for each other and their passion for their work.

During his final battle with cancer, Marty told a friend: "I think the most important thing I've done is to enable Ruth to do what she has done."[64]

On Building and Maintaining Friendships

RUTH BADER GINSBURG DIDN'T GROW up with the dream of becoming a lawyer. In fact, she's said that if she could have been anything in life, she would've "been a diva." But her grade school music teacher didn't think she had what it took (she was a sparrow, not a robin) and told her to never sing the words, just mouth them instead.[1]

Why am I telling you this story in a chapter about relationships? First, because it made me laugh when I heard Ginsburg tell it onstage in December 2018 (and I, too, have not gotten over the low performance review my grade school music teacher gave me). More importantly, because though the Notorious RBG never became a glorious singer, she is featured in an opera. Well, she and the other justice who also wanted to be a diva,[2] the late Antonin Scalia. The two shared a love for Brooklyn (where they were both born), opera, travel, and the law. Though the justices did not always see eye to eye on the law, their fierce friendship is one for the books.

"I love him, but sometimes I'd like to strangle him," Ginsburg once said of Justice Scalia.[3]

There is a lot to learn from the way the justice treats the people in her life, both on the court and off. She has impeccable manners, she listens (like really, truly listens) and thinks before she speaks, she helps other people without hesitation, and she sends handwritten thank-you notes. In today's political climate, it often feels impossible to befriend or date or eat dinner near someone who has differing political ideas. However, Ginsburg's way of life provides two important reminders. The first is to find ways to connect with people, no matter the difference in opinion. The second is to be there for those you care about.

PART I: The Court

There are many people out there who questioned Ginsburg and Scalia's friendship, which began when they worked together in the 1980s at the US Court of Appeals for the DC Circuit, but the proof of their adoration for each other is clear. They just "clicked."[4] The two took vacations together, where they rode elephants, they spent New Year's Eve together (Scalia would kill the meat, Marty would cook it[5]), they went to the opera, they edited each other's opposite opinions, you name it. Scalia brought her roses on her birthday, and Ginsburg called Scalia a "discerning shopper."[6] Though the duo had differing thoughts when it came to matters of the law—Ginsburg goes left while Scalia went far right—the two cared deeply for each other.

Steven Calabresi, a professor at Northwestern University School of Law and cofounder of the Federalist Society, the conservative lawyers' group, told *The New Yorker* in 2013 that he was enticed by Ginsburg's time on the DC Circuit mainly because, even though it was clear she disagreed with the other judges on certain topics, she was able to maintain friendships with them.[7]

Ginsburg has always been a big fan of challenging her more conservative colleagues.[8] Scalia felt the same way about her liberal counterparts—in fact, his son once said Scalia would think less of someone who couldn't spar intellectually with him.[9]

"I interviewed Justice Scalia once and he said that their friendship was just predicated by the fact that she was the smartest person he knew and I think she would say he was one of the smartest people she knew," journalist Dahlia Lithwick said to me on the phone.

"And also, she thought he was hilarious," added Lithwick. This is true—Ginsburg has called Scalia's sense of humor "infectious."[10]

"He'd sit next to me and he'd whisper something or hand me a note that would crack me up and [I did] all I could do to avoid breaking out into hysterical laughter," Ginsburg said two years after Scalia's death.[11]

Their friendship was no doubt pure—to the chagrin of Ginsburg's feminist friends and fans—but there is an underlying truth coursing beneath all relationships held between members of the court: the institution comes first.

"I think that the principal value for her is the institution comes first, the esteem of the institution," said Lithwick.

In Ginsburg's mind, you can have differing opinions than someone else, but more importantly, you also have a job to do.

"All of us appreciate that the institution we serve is far more important than the particular individuals who compose the Court's bench at any given time. And our job, in my view, is the best work a jurist anywhere could have," Ginsburg has said. "Our charge is to pursue justice as best we can."[12]

While neither of them shied away from disagreeing with each other, Ginsburg and Scalia considered it part of their job, as either a lawyer or a judge, to share their views frankly, but to avoid making it personal. The two separately understood they could not afford to do that, Antonin Scalia's son Eugene said once to CNN. He also said their differences in some ways actually bolstered their friendship.[13]

Anyone who loves RBG knows about this odd relationship with a man who seemed to always disagree with her (I actually often overheard this friendship discussed at bars when I lived in Washington, DC). As Ginsburg's fame grew, more attention was paid to it, and eventually, composer-librettist Derrick Wang wrote a duet for Scalia and Ginsburg titled "We Are Different, We Are One." Ginsburg once explained that difference comes from the way they interpret legal texts, but they are one because of their shared reverence for the Constitution and the US judiciary that they serve.[14] Collegiality on the court is necessary in order for the justices to do the challenging job assigned to them.[15]

Ginsburg is not the only justice who holds the institution above all else. In fact, the idea seems widely held by all justices who take a seat at the Supreme Court. Though it may seem like each justice exists in his or her own universe, everyone remains considerate, polite, and friendly, even if there are not strong friendships.[16]

"I think that's the institution," NPR's legal correspondent Nina Totenberg said to me on the phone. "It's like marriage for life." So even if people don't actually like other members of the court, "they try to bury that, they have to live together for the rest of their lives. There's no divorce here."

Since women seem to always be in charge of making and keeping the peace, who else would Ginsburg credit most for promoting collegiality among the court's members but the first woman on the Supreme Court, the honorable Sandra Day O'Connor? She is not the only one who shines a light on O'Connor's efforts. Justice Stephen Breyer also credited O'Connor with this, once writing, "Sandra has a special talent, perhaps a gene, for lighting up the room . . . she enters it; for [restoring] good humor in the presence of strong disagreement; for [producing constructive results; and for [reminding] those at odds today . . . that 'tomorrow is another day.'"[17]

★ ★ ★

Speaking of odd couples of the Supreme Court, Ginsburg and O'Connor could not be more different (though multiple sources made sure to talk about how they were both drop-dead gorgeous, not that it matters). Ginsburg grew up in Brooklyn, O'Connor on a Texas ranch; Ginsburg was small, O'Connor tall; Ginsburg leaned liberal while O'Connor leaned conservative. In fact, O'Connor's votes diverged more from Ginsburg's than from any other justice besides the late Justice John Paul

Stevens.[18] Despite these differences, the two watched out for one another, because they were more effective together than apart. Before Ginsburg joined the court, O'Connor had taken more clerks from Ginsburg's chambers than from any other federal judge on all the courts below.[19]

After Ginsburg's cancer surgery in 1999, O'Connor was the first person to call her. O'Connor had fought breast cancer while on the bench and was calling to tell RBG about dealing with cancer while on the court.[20] She explained to Ginsburg that the best plan would be to have her chemotherapy on Friday so that Ginsburg would have the weekend to recover before the court's session on Monday.[21] This is what Ginsburg did for the next eight months, and it is likely a part of why she didn't miss any meetings—though it's important to note that O'Connor was not the only justice who helped her, as RBG has said that everyone on the court took care of her during that tough time.[22]

"Her welcome when I became the junior justice is characteristic," said Ginsburg at an awards ceremony honoring O'Connor. She explained that there are customs and habits of the court not officially recorded, but known. "Justice O'Connor knew what it was like to learn the ropes on one's own. She told me what I needed to know when I came on board for the court's 1993 term—not an intimidating dose, just enough to enable me to navigate safely my first days and weeks."[23]

Ginsburg frequently tells the story about getting her first opinion assignment. She was expecting to be assigned an uncontroversial, unanimous decision, as was tradition. But the chief justice gave her a very detailed and definitely not easy case. O'Connor had simple advice for the newbie: just get it done. The veteran justice also told Ginsburg to circulate her draft opinion before the next set of assignments was made. If she didn't, she risked getting another strenuous case.[24]

The message behind this advice was simple: Ginsburg had a job to do, and it was not worth it to waste time on emotions such as anger or resentment.[25] This advice might sound familiar to those who know Ginsburg now—it is similar to what she has said about anger and persuasion on the court herself.

And this idea has impacted even Ginsburg's granddaughter, Clara Spera, who wrote about what it was like to be RBG's relative in an essay for *Glamour*.

"But her work and friendships—like with the late Justice Antonin Scalia—have inspired me to listen to those I may disagree with and to find areas where we can build together," Spera said.[26]

★ ★ ★

Ginsburg has acknowledged that justices can put aside their own egos for the court[27] and has explained how the collegiality found among justices is purposefully fostered. All routine gatherings between the justices begin with handshakes, and they all have lunch together in the Justices' Dining Room on days when they either meet to discuss cases or on days they hear arguments.

There is no rule saying the justices have to eat together; they do so by choice. Though sometimes it includes all nine, usually six to eight justices can be found dining together.[28] Retired justices will also sometimes join them, like Justice O'Connor. Conversation topics vary but might include lawyers' performance in the cases heard that term, a new production in town, exhibitions at DC museums, or the justices' children and grandchildren. Before his death, Scalia would lead the chorus of "Happy Birthday" when they were celebrating a birthday, and when a new justice joins the rank, it is the duty of the former junior justice to arrange a welcome dinner for all the justices.[29] The spouses (until 1981 it was always wives) of Supreme Court justices also formed a sense of comradery. They would all have lunch together three times a year.[30]

While giving a speech on the lighter side of the Supreme Court, Ginsburg joked that the public may have noticed the justices have severe differences on topics like affirmative action, the Second Amendment, immigration, or federally mandated health care. Yet they really do—no joke—enjoy each other's company, and their mutual respect for each other holds strong throughout these disagreements about what the law is or should be.[31]

★ ★ ★

I remember when one of my roommates came back to our four-person house on H Street NE in Washington, DC. It was 2014, and RBG's dissents had become famous. I had recently seen a talk between Justice Ginsburg and Justice Scalia and had been surprised by how pure their friendship was, and how he got Justice Ginsburg to crack a smile, even when they were debating onstage. That day, I was sitting on the couch in the kitchen when my roommate pulled out a little mouse toy for our new kitten, Ruth Bader Ginsburg, to play with. The mouse's name? Antonin Scalia. Why? I don't remember the exact wording, but the general idea was that Ruthie, as we called the cat, was going to bat him all over the place.

Clearly, Ginsburg does not always agree with her colleagues. This is why she started speaking her mind from the bench, reading dissents striking enough to capture the nation's attention. So how can we all incorporate this idea into our lives of not ignoring those with whom we disagree but instead following RBG's example and inviting them to a respectful discussion? Focus on your ultimate goals.

A few of Ginsburg's clerks all reiterated a similar idea to me: Ginsburg cared most about her work and therefore focused her energy on that.

"I think she would say that maintaining personal animosities and holding grudges and staying angry are all things that ultimately diminish *you*, rather than the other person, and they keep you from being sufficiently clear and focused on what your long-term goals are for yourself and for the world," said Paul Schiff Berman, who clerked for Ginsburg from 2001 to 2002.

Ruthanne Deutsch, who clerked for the justice in 2007–2008, said that Ginsburg focuses "on objective results" and doesn't "personalize things." Meanwhile, Elizabeth Porter, who clerked in 2002–2003, said, "Her brilliant legal work, her ability to get along with people with whom she disagrees, her inspirationally romantic marriage, and even her love of opera and art all reflect her focus on the essence of things."

It is also possible that her ability to create these friendships is proof of a different world. Heather Elliott, who clerked in 2001–2002, said that she guesses Ginsburg "had no choice but to learn how to get along with people who disagreed with her" due to her time fighting for gender equality.

Lithwick said that though Ginsburg's friendship with Scalia was very intense, very deep, and very layered, it also came about because it was a function of the time.

"I don't think she had the same luxury to say, 'Every man that pisses me off is dead to me,' because she would've been alone on an island with Marty," she said during our phone interview. "I think she had no option to go in guns blazing because she wouldn't have done anything [otherwise]."

Ginsburg is incredibly pragmatic. Therefore, in order to be successful at law school, while teaching, while litigating, or while on the bench, Ginsburg couldn't hold grudges against those with whom she disagreed.

"I think if she carried around the grudges and resentment . . . going back to Harvard Law School, she would not have been able to function, and I think she just made a calculation very early on that she was not going to be a creature of like a multitude of resentment and that instead she was just going to be effective," Lithwick said.

★ ★ ★

These days, people can, and do, divide themselves strictly on party or idea lines. There have been articles about conservatives having trouble finding dates[32] or how to avoid talking about politics during the holidays so that there are not screaming matches over the dinner table. Even in 2019 and the years ahead, it is still possible to take a page out of Ginsburg's book, and find ways to connect with people, no matter the difference in opinion.

"In this day and age, we tend to think that how you feel about immigration or something defines you as a person," said David Post, who twice clerked for Ginsburg, first when she was on the DC Circuit and then again when she was on the Supreme Court. "If I take a different position than you take, you sort of write me off as a person. And maybe that's right, there's a lot of that going on, there's two war camps and it extends to every possible idea and every possible perspective and all the rest, to focus on the differences. The Scalia thing focused on their commonalities, they had a lot in common and they knew that, and they enjoyed each other's company too much to let it get spoiled by very serious disagreements about very important things."

Post said that the "moral of the Scalia friendship story" is that "work is work, the world of ideas is a challenging one," but at the end of the day, "you can connect with people because they're New Yorkers or you like baseball, you can connect with people in a lot of different ways." Post told me that he thinks Ginsburg's relationships with Scalia and O'Connor "enriched" the lives of those involved. There are always going to be ways to connect, and not every disagreement is worth ruining a relationship over.

Of course, Ginsburg never compromised her beliefs to fit Scalia's or anyone else's—part of the fun of their friendship, it seems, is that their disagreements actually made the other person's arguments stronger. Scalia would pinpoint the weakest spots of Ginsburg's argument, allowing Ginsburg to strengthen them.[33] For example, take the *VMI* case, which is likely Ginsburg's most important majority opinion. Scalia made sure he gave RBG his dissent a little early so that she could respond to it in her opinion.[34] This is a great example of both civility and neither of them sacrificing their beliefs for the other.

Scott Dodson, a lawyer and the editor of *The Legacy of Ruth Bader Ginsburg*, told me that part of these friendships with people who have opposing views is possible because Ginsburg "knows herself and she has a very thick skin," which allows her to brush off things that she disagrees with or is upset by, and can instead focus on what she loves about the person.

"That's something that I think is really important for every person, to have productive working relationships and social relationships, is just being able to see what you really like in people and value them for that," Dodson said. "I think that's really important even if you disagree with them on philosophical or political issues."

PART II: Friendships Outside the Court

Obviously, Ginsburg has other friends than the feistiest conservative justice from the bench. Ginsburg is incredibly close to many members of the press, as well. She still keeps in touch with the women and men she worked with as an advocate and litigator, and she remains friends with her clients as well. Her clerks become family. All of this is to say that Ginsburg values relationships and friendships, and seems to go above and beyond in order to make people feel valued, respected, and heard.

Before Ginsburg even had the opportunity to forge friendships on the Supreme Court, she was a teacher. A pretty boring one, according to some of her former students. Frank Askin, her student while at Rutgers and then her colleague at the university and also the ACLU, told me that when he took Ginsburg's civil procedure class his first year, it was "was basically a conversation between Ruth and me; the other students were out of it" because they were bored.

Askin told me a story that Ruth herself has told too—
at the end of one year, the Rutgers students put on a skit.
One student, meant to be Ginsburg, is quietly lecturing on
"something or other" and somebody behind her is stripping
"Ginsburg's" clothes off and she's totally oblivious, and she's
suddenly standing there in her underwear, still lecturing.
Luckily for the students, Ginsburg found it "hilarious."

Nevertheless, the essence of teaching itself—people
learning about the law and how to write well—stayed with
Ginsburg, and she brought it to her time at the DC Circuit
and the Supreme Court. Ginsburg's former clerk, Heather
Elliott, said that Ginsburg remains a "tremendous teacher"
and told me about the first time she wrote a bench memo for
Ginsburg, claiming that it "wasn't particularly good."

"She marked it up like a professor would have, and she
sat down with me for an hour to go over what approach she
wanted me to take in the future," Elliott said. "Obviously some
of that is for her own benefit (getting better bench memos in
the future), but it was a lot for me, too—she wanted me to
learn from my mistakes and her (vastly greater) experience,
and I did."

Her time as a professor shines through how she works as a
judge. Herma Kay Hill, the late iconic professor who worked
with Ginsburg during the 1970s, wrote in *The Legacy of Ruth
Bader Ginsburg* that the link between Justice Ginsburg and
Professor Ginsburg is very clear.[35] Justice Ginsburg sharpens
the law while breaking new ground. Meanwhile, Professor
Ginsburg helps people understand how these decisions all lay a
foundation for future cases.[36]

Ginsburg's life as a law professor allowed her to set an
example of how to meld real-world advocacy with classroom

teaching. She utilized these skills on the bench when trying to further progressive issues. Kay Hill wrote that Ginsburg will continue to inspire other women to believe in and act upon their personal and professional goals. But her biggest contribution to the nation does not rely on her sex, but instead on her "thoroughly documented and carefully articulated opinions."[37]

★ ★ ★

We can always learn how to be better friends and mentors to those in our lives. One tip from Heather Elliott, a former clerk, is to not let the little things bother you. Ginsburg instead "focuses on what matters." This is shown in multiple ways, and one pretty simple way is that she doesn't care how her clerks are dressed (unless they are in attendance in the courtroom) and that she does not care about them adhering to her schedule, as long as they get their work done.

For example, Elliott said that other justices require their clerks to wear suits every day, and that though this may seem like an inconsequential point, it's "illustrative of the larger one: keep focused on what's important." You don't need to be wearing a pantsuit to write a brief.

"An anecdote to illustrate: when I started my clerkship, I asked the outgoing clerk who I overlapped with about the dress code, and he said, 'She doesn't care.' And I thought, *Right—she's so stylish, how can she not care?*" Elliott told me in an email interview. "But the next day, he said, 'The justice is here, let's go say hi,' and he was wearing the *most* disgusting workout clothes you have ever seen (shorts that were too short, muscle tee cut to expose his midriff, rotten sneakers). And we went into the justice's office, and she didn't blink an eye."

Multiple clerks also talked about how lenient the justice was about family matters—and she especially liked it when it was fathers who needed to take care of their children. RBG remembers what it was like to be a mother and a young lawyer, and therefore has always been understanding about her clerks leaving to pick up their kids or coming in late after dropping them off.

David Post explained to me that law was a second career for him, and he had spent time as the primary parent while his wife worked. This made him "desirable" to Ginsburg when he got into law, because as we all know, the perfect world includes fathers sharing equal parenting duties with mothers. As long as Post completed the work she needed him to get done, Ginsburg was always understanding of him rushing off to tend to the needs of his kids.

"In terms of my time, she didn't make allowances, but it was 'Get your work done, I don't care, just get your work done,'" he said. "She was very results-oriented."

Former clerk Ryan Park wrote a story for *The Atlantic* about how The Boss, a common nickname clerks call their justice while working at the court, taught him a lot of lessons about being a stay-at-home dad because of the way she navigated family and career obstacles with "deftness and grace." Ginsburg told Park to "be a good partner" and "take breaks," leading him to take a short break from his law career after his clerkship so that he could be the primary caregiver to his young daughter.[38]

★ ★ ★

It can be easy to forget that the Notorious RBG has a life outside of her chambers and off the bench, but she does, and it is apparent that she cares deeply for the people who exist in her world. She doesn't just build these friendships with people on the court or with her clerks because she thinks she should—deep down, the justice is just out-of-this-world kind.

"She's incredibly considerate of people. If she's been to dinner at your house, no matter how many times she's been to dinner, [you] get a note," journalist Nina Totenberg told me. "If you're one of her law clerks and you have a baby or there's a marriage of your children, you get a note. Everybody gets notes. If you're her doctor, you get a note; in a difficult time, you get a note."

In *The Legacy of Ruth Bader Ginsburg,* Totenberg wrote about their friendship, saying Ginsburg was a very generous friend, especially when Totenberg's late husband was very sick for nearly five years. RBG would pick up Totenberg and take her somewhere to try to cheer her up.[39]

Once you're in her life, it seems pretty clear that you stay there. Multiple clerks told me that there has never been a time where they've written to their former boss and didn't get some sort of response back. This is an impressive feat for someone who probably gets more fan mail than anyone else on the Supreme Court (all of which she also tries to respond to).

David Post told me a touching story about when he was clerking for her while she was on the court. His father was really sick, and Ginsburg knew that. Without telling David, she sent his parents a handwritten note about how great David was, how she couldn't do it without him, and how proud she was of him.

She knew that it would mean a lot to them and that it would "bowl them over" to receive this handwritten note.

Post said it was an incredibly nice thing for Ginsburg to do, but it was also something that came naturally to her—she knew it would mean a lot to his parents, so she did it. Sometimes what might be the simplest thing for you to do will mean the most to those you care about, and who care about you.

Kate Andrias, now a professor at the University of Michigan Law School, clerked for Ginsburg in the 2006 term. There are five of Ginsburg's former clerks at the school, and so one year before she came to speak, the university made a video of the clerks talking about what they learned from her and how they would describe her. Andrias said Justice Ginsburg made sure to pause and celebrate, with trips to the opera or maybe a cake on a special day, despite the endless amount of work at the court. She was an "absolutely wonderful boss."[40]

Schlanger, who was originally hired to clerk for Ginsburg on the DC Circuit and then was among Ginsburg's first group of law clerks at the Supreme Court, is also a professor at the University of Michigan.

"RBG is an amazing presence," Schlanger said when asked to describe the justice. She said after working for RBG, you will want to live up to her dedication, smarts, and drive for the rest of your career. This stage is set day one of clerking for her.[41]

Schlanger also talks about how after her clerkship ended, she played a concert performance of *The Magic Flute*. Not only did Ruth Bader Ginsburg come to see it, she brought the rest of the chambers with her.[42]

★ ★ ★

We've all been there—blurting out an idea or thought or sentence before really thinking it through. Think about how many times you've said, "You too" in response to the person who takes your movie ticket (but is definitely not seeing the movie) telling you, "Enjoy the show." Well, Ruth Bader Ginsburg might not understand this feeling. She is the living example of thinking before you speak. She doesn't mind silence or lengthy pauses. In fact, her clerks actually have what they call the "two-Mississippi rule: after speaking, wait two beats before you say anything else."[43] Dahlia Lithwick explained that this is not an "age thing," as some people might think, but is just the way she is, and if as an interviewer you rush forward in that silence and ask a question, you miss the second round of thought where "[Ginsburg] says the really new considerate thing." It can be uncomfortable to wait out that pause, but you do it because you know what's coming will be good.

Journalist Marvin Kalb talked about the first time he ever met Ginsburg. They met at a mutual friend's home, and Kalb "made a point of talking, perhaps a little more than I should have," because he was trying to get her to engage in conversation.

"I failed," Kalb states during our phone interview. "And the following day I called my host and hostess and I said, 'I must've failed with the justice because I couldn't get her to participate, and [the hostess] said, 'She heard everything you said, she didn't have anything to add to the discussion so she said nothing.' That struck me as interesting, because in Washington, people are talking constantly, whether they have something to add or not."

That classic saying, "Think before you speak," is really how Ginsburg lives her life. But that means that when she does speak, people really listen.

"Maybe if you're quiet, people sometimes listen to what you have to say more intensely, they lean in and pay attention, because you're thinking and you're saying exactly what you want . . . a little bit of hypnosis in a way," said Post.

★ ★ ★

When I started writing this book, I assumed I would learn a lot about how to work hard and create positive change through a career, and I figured that because of the work she did, Ruth Bader Ginsburg was likely a pretty good person. I did learn all that, but hearing all the stories about the above-and-beyond kindness and sensitivity the justice shows to everyone in her life—whether she diverges from them on ideological grounds or not—has been a surprise and a pleasure.

I have also learned that I wish my manners were as good as the justice's, and I am going to remember that next time I don't want to write a thank-you note. But I want to end this chapter with the overarching message that I see as most important: We would all be better off at least hearing each other out and trying to really listen to each other, regardless of differences, to see where we can create bonds. In today's climate, it is easy to dismiss others immediately, and I am sure we're all guilty of it. It is worth remembering that friendships can be forged based on commonalities and respect and mutual understanding of the institution you serve (whatever that may be), and that sometimes friendships that challenge you ultimately make your own beliefs stronger. Besides, you never know where a new lifelong friendship might spring from.

5

On the Shoulders We Stand On

Barbara babcock met ruth bader Ginsburg for the first time in the early 1970s, when they were both among a very small number of female law professors, Babcock at Stanford and Ginsburg at Rutgers. At the time, women law professors were "as rare as unicorns," Babcock told me, and so they all knew each other, either personally or by reputation. Babcock's career trajectory was similar to that of Ginsburg—she, too, had struggled to find a job even though she was very smart, and they were both asked by female law students to teach a course on women and the law (Babcock at Georgetown and Ginsburg at Rutgers).

While Babcock and Ginsburg weren't particularly close friends, they were doing the same thing and therefore knew that they could count on each other. At the time, Babcock didn't think that Ginsburg's efforts in women's equality would place her at the top of their shared profession, but she admired the courage Ginsburg displayed in throwing herself entirely into the movement and litigation. But Babcock forgot to factor in one thing: Marty Ginsburg. Marty called and asked Babcock for help when Ruth Ginsburg was being considered for appointment on the DC Circuit. At the time, Babcock was Assistant to the Attorney General for the Civil Division, and Attorney General Griffin Bell had asked her to find some women for the president to appoint to federal courts.

Without hesitation, Babcock wrote to the Attorney General and explained that "for this very visible appointment that could lead to the Supreme Court, it had to be Ruth."

"I cannot exaggerate the feeling among women lawyers that all increases in numbers or victories are pyrrhic if Ruth is not appointed," she wrote to Bell. She told him it would be a "slap in the face" if Ruth, who not only was more qualified than "any woman applicant in the country" but had also absolutely paid her dues, was not chosen.

Bell proceeded to recommend Ginsburg, and the rest is history. According to Babcock, who is a professor emerita at Stanford Law School, since that moment, Ginsburg has always given her "tremendous credit" for helping at that time. This seems to come as a surprise to Babcock when she talks about how much credit Ginsburg has and continues to give her.

"I just thought, she doesn't have to do that, nobody knows except Marty and a few others that I was such a big help to her, and I only did it out of duty, I felt as though we owed it to her, and that nobody else would've given up their highest ambitions to help the movement the way she did," Babcock said in a phone interview. Babcock explained that she doesn't believe Ginsburg would have ever called her to ask for help, because she wouldn't think Babcock owed her anything. It was all Marty. But because Babcock did help, she will always be thanked.

This is a theme in Ginsburg's life: acknowledging those whose shoulders she stands on to get to where she is. The lesson here is pretty straightforward: no one does anything alone and we should all acknowledge that, both in the moment and as we move forward. Be sure to frequently (and loudly) thank those who either paved the way or helped us along the path.

"She is always just very scrupulously careful to say, 'I stand on the shoulders of the people who came before me,'" said journalist Dahlia Lithwick.

For example, Babcock was invited in 2018 to give the annual Justice Ruth Ginsburg Distinguished Lecture on Women and the Law at the City Bar in New York—a "very prestigious" event. Babcock went with her husband.

"[Ruth] gave me the warmest, sweetest introduction, I mean it was really, it was almost motherly, of all the things that I had done for her and for so many other women. I was knocked down," Babcock told me. "There were things that I didn't know she knew even about me. Honestly, there's no other word for it but sweet."

★ ★ ★

Though Ruth Bader Ginsburg deserves endless accolades for the work she did in changing laws surrounding gender equality, she did not do it alone—and she is usually the first to acknowledge that. We all have people in our life who helped us get to where we are or who paved the way before we even began. Nearly forty years after Babcock played a supporting role to RBG's success, Babcock is still touched that Ginsburg acknowledges that helping hand. We can all make sure the people who helped us in our lives feel as honored as Babcock does.

The four women who have sat on the Supreme Court all seem to take this lesson to heart, and each has taken a turn supporting each other, like when O'Connor helped Ginsburg through her cancer treatments or when Justice Elena Kagan, the fourth woman nominated to the Supreme Court, talked about how Ginsburg paved Kagan's own road to the court.

"More than any other person, she can take credit for making the law of this country work for women," she has said.[1]

Ginsburg's thanks, acknowledgment, and uplifting of the women who are important to her, both in the past and in the present, means that she has a support system when she in turn needs it. Sonia Sotomayor, in turn, was there for Ginsburg during an incredibly hard point in the older justice's life. Journalist Joan Biskupic wrote a book about Sotomayor, and in it, tells the story of the court's end-of-term party the year Marty died. Sotomayor put on salsa music, and went over to RBG, who was sitting quietly off to the side of the event. Marty had died just days before. Sotomayor whispered to Ruth that her husband would've wanted her to get up and dance. Biskupic writes, "Ginsburg relented and followed Sotomayor in a few steps. Ginsburg put her hands up to Sotomayor's face. Holding her two cheeks in her palms, Ginsburg said, 'Thank you.'"[2]

★ ★ ★

When Ginsburg's nephew, Daniel Stiepleman, wanted to make a movie about his aunt's life, the justice had two requests: she wanted the law to be depicted accurately, and she did not want viewers to think that she shattered legal barriers alone, "as if it had never occurred to anyone else that women should be considered equal."[3]

"She said, 'I built my career on the shoulders of women who came before me, like Dorothy Kenyon, like Pauli Murray, and people should know that,'" Stiepleman told the *New York Times* during an interview in 2018.[4] He said that he then wrote Kenyon, a pioneering feminist social activist and lawyer, into the script.[5]

While living in Sweden, Ginsburg learned about the word "vägmärken," which translates to "way paver" or "pathmaker,"[6] and she likes to use those terms to pay tribute to those who put in the work years before she did. Even in her earliest briefs with the ACLU, Ginsburg would be sure to note the contributions her students made or would be sure to illuminate little-known historical figures who had contributed to the fight long before Ginsburg herself did.[7] For example, on the brief she wrote for *Reed v. Reed*, Ginsburg credited Kenyon and Murray as coauthors, though neither woman had written a single word of the brief. Kenyon had been arguing for equal treatment of women since 1917, while Murray was the great-granddaughter of an enslaved person and a slaveholder. Professor Linda K. Kerber credits Murray in *The Legacy of Ruth Bader Ginsburg* with doing more than nearly anyone else in her generation to link racism with sexism.[8]

Ginsburg listed Kenyon and Murray because she was ahead of her time in understanding that she had a debt to the women who fought for equality the generations before. Kerber explains that RBG knew she would never successfully challenge old laws if Kenyon and Murray, and many others, had not begun the battle years before.[9]

It has been noted that Ginsburg started using the term "gender discrimination" when she was arguing in front of the Supreme Court in the 1970s because repeating the word "sex" in front of nine men might not have been the best plan and might have led to wandering minds. However, Ginsburg didn't originally think of this, and she is always sure to give credit to her secretary at Columbia, who told Ginsburg to make the change. Ginsburg's secretary was typing up endless briefs and articles that contained the word "sex." She finally voiced her concern to Ginsburg, saying, "Don't you know that those nine men (on the Supreme Court)—they hear that word, and their first association is not the way you want them to be thinking? Why don't you use the word gender? It is a grammatical term and it will ward off distracting associations."[10]

Over the years, Ginsburg has either received awards or been asked to speak at awards ceremonies. She frequently uses her time onstage to talk about other way pavers.

Take, for example, the time that Ginsburg was giving a speech at the Annual Conference of the National Association of Women Judges in 1995 in Georgia, and she spent the whole time talking about some "great ladies,"[11] including Judges Florence Ellinwood Allen, Burnita Shelton Matthews, and Shirley Mount Hufstedler, who were among the first females to gain a seat on the federal bench. They served with "extraordinary devotion and distinction," and along with other women of the time, helped make it "less difficult for the rest of us to gain appointment or election to the judiciary, and realistic for legions of women in the future to aspire to—and achieve—a full life in the law."[12]

Then there was the time she received the Rita C. Davidson Award (the highest award given by the Women's Bar Association of Maryland). During her acceptance speech, Ginsburg spoke highly of Davidson, who was the first woman to serve on the Maryland Court of Appeals, and acknowledged that Davidson used her skills to try to make the world a better place for those not in the majority.[13] Then Ginsburg took it one step further, and dedicated the rest of her speaking time to tell the story of Belva Ann Lockwood, who knocked down many legal glass ceilings, becoming the first woman to argue a case in front of the Supreme Court, the first woman to gain admission to the Supreme Court's bar, and the first woman to appear on official ballots for president.[14]

Time and again she uses her position of power and prestige to give credit to those who allowed a Jewish woman to eventually sit on the highest court in the land. Lithwick once wrote a book review of *My Own Words,* the biography written by Ginsburg, Wendy W. Williams, and Mary Hartnett, for the *Washington Post,* in which she pointed out that Ginsburg's "life's work has been to use law to make the invisible seen."[15]

The review also calls out one section of the work, where Ginsburg questions the difference between a New York City garment district bookkeeper and a Supreme Court justice. She answers her own question by saying that the difference is a generation's worth of opportunities that were available to her but not her mother.[16]

"Even at her confirmation hearing, even when she was sworn in, she named the Harriet Tubmans and the women who came before," Lithwick said to me, "and I think what she is saying, is that this kind of story that we tell of like, her greatness, is not the story, and that the story is she achieved what she achieved because amazing men and women gave her opportunities."

Lithwick is referring to Ginsburg's nomination speech in the White House Rose Garden, when she said, "The increasingly full use of the talent of all of this nation's people holds large promise for the future, but we could not have come to this point—and I surely would not be in this room today—without the determined efforts of men and women who kept dreams of equal citizenship alive in days when few would listen."[17] She goes on to name Susan B. Anthony, Elizabeth Cady Stanton, and Harriet Tubman before saying, "I stand on the shoulders of those brave people."[18] She also thanked the women's movement for opening doors for her, and the civil rights movement of the 1960s, because the women's movement drew inspiration from it.[19]

Finally, Ginsburg used that moment in the Rose Garden to pay tribute to her mother, who not only was taken too soon, but was never offered the same opportunities Ruth was. Still, Celia pushed her daughter to grow and learn in the hopes that she would have a different life.

"I pray that I may be all that she would have been, had she lived in an age when women could aspire and achieve, and daughters are cherished as much as sons,"[20] the nominee said in June 1993. After Ruth finished, Clinton wiped away tears.

★ ★ ★

On top of all this, as the second woman nominated to the Supreme Court, Ginsburg always makes sure to honor the first. She has said that she could barely keep up with the pace Justice Sandra Day O'Connor set.[21]

During a speech honoring O'Connor, Ginsburg tells the tale of how after Ginsburg wrote her first opinion, O'Connor gave her a note that read, "This is your first opinion for the Court, it is a fine one, I look forward to many more."[22] The note made Ginsburg feel so good that she went on to send similar notes to Justice Sotomayor and Justice Kagan after they gave their first opinions for the court.

O'Connor was consistently there for Ginsburg, even though they had differing views of the law. To give just one example, let's look at the *Virginia Military Institute (VMI)* opinion. Only Chief Justice Rehnquist and Justice Scalia supported *VMI*, which wanted to keep women from attending their all-male school. The other six justices voted that the school should admit women, and O'Connor was to write the opinion. In her book *Sisters in Law,* Linda Hirshman explains O'Connor turned around and said, "This should be Ruth's."[23] Ginsburg used this opportunity to "blur" the difference between the higher standard of review for race discrimination and the lower standard for sex discrimination.[24] O'Connor gave her the opportunity to write this very important opinion, knowing that Ginsburg had spent decades working toward the standard the *VMI* decision now set.

Ginsburg continues to make sure that everyone knows these stories about Justice O'Connor. She is also always careful to note the discrimination and discouragement that her "colleague and counselor" faced, and consistently cites O'Connor as the "source for her stories about the difference women can make."[25]

"As women achieve power, the barriers will fall," Ginsburg remembers O'Connor telling her. "As society sees what women can do, as women see what women can do, there will be more women out there doing things, and we'll all be better off for it."[26]

Ginsburg took this message to heart. Before O'Connor left, and then during her lonely years as the only woman, the second female justice would frequently highlight the positive impact having two women on the bench brought to viewers of the court. During their time together on the court, which amounted to nearly twelve and a half years, young people were able to see that women speak differently than each other, and hold differing opinions, just like men do. Ginsburg likes to talk about how throughout their shared time on the court, lawyers presenting their case kept calling the two female justices by each other's names. So the National Association of Women Judges had T-shirts made for the two of them. Justice O'Connor's shirt said, "I'm Sandra, not Ruth," and Ginsburg's read, "I'm Ruth, not Sandra."[27]

RBG's former clerk Paul Schiff Berman told me a story that illustrates why it is important to acknowledge the shoulders we all stand on. He said while he was clerking for RBG, a group of Girl Scouts came to tour the Supreme Court. He remembered a relatively young girl asking Ginsburg if she had always wanted to be a Supreme Court justice.

"[Ginsburg] gave this very twinkly smile and said, 'You know, you have to understand that when I was your age, the idea that I would even become a lawyer, that anyone would ever hire me as a lawyer, was not at all obvious, so the idea of being a judge or a Supreme Court justice was not even on the horizon,'" Berman recalled. "And I think she loved hearing that question because she loves the fact that a young girl today can think 'Oh, I want to be a Supreme Court justice' in a way that was not possible when she was that age."

By consistently acknowledging the women who came before her, Ruth Bader Ginsburg is showing us that we can all aim to be and do whatever we want, because we have many examples of people to follow. RBG and O'Connor showed us that women with different ideas and interests can have the same job and both excel. Ginsburg makes sure we never forget that.

After O'Connor left the bench, Ginsburg sat alone, missing her friend.

"The word I would use to describe my position on the bench is 'lonely,'" she said the year after O'Connor left. "This is how it was for Sandra's first twelve years. Neither of us ever thought this would happen again."[28]

She continued, saying that though the justices had very different lives growing up and were repeatedly divided on key legal questions, the two had "the experience of growing up women and we have certain sensitivities that our male colleagues lack."[29] Ginsburg never realized how much she would miss her friend until she was gone.[30]

★ ★ ★

In Ginsburg's world, acknowledging those on whose shoulders she stands does not just mean looking backwards and honoring those who came before. It also means actively lifting up those who are fighting the good fight at the same time. The justice is known to talk about the work other women are doing at the same time as her, and I heard story after story about her being a good, loyal friend to the people in her life and to the work she has done.

For example, I was told about a time when a friend of Ginsburg's was blackballed by a famous formerly all-male club in Washington, DC. Years later, Ginsburg was asked to join the club and was given a tour. But instead of joining, she told them, "Well it's a very beautiful club, but if it's too good for [my friend], it's too good for me." She wasn't willing to let a club walk all over someone whom she admired and cared for.

Or there's the time period right after she was nominated by President Clinton to take a seat on the Supreme Court. She spent that summer meeting with members of Capital Hill and going through the hearing process. Robert Katzmann, who was helping Ginsburg prepare for these meetings and hearings, said that then–Judge Ginsburg never tried to hide her past work.

RBG would not distance herself from her time with the Women's Rights Project, the ACLU, or any of her past work as a litigator, even when she was directly asked in meetings with senators or during her hearing. Ginsburg understood that she would be challenged on these beliefs while standing alone, facing the panel, and she was ready to face that challenge head-on. In *The Legacy of Ruth Bader Ginsburg,* Katzmann calls this a "testament to her principles and loyalty."[31]

★ ★ ★

Honoring those whose shoulders we stand on teaches younger generations that they can pursue dreams, they can dissent, they can break down barriers, they can create change, because of the path that has been paved for them by those who came before.

They can (and oftentimes should) do it differently, and do it their own way, but by talking about those who tried so hard to tear down barriers, we show that anything is possible. It also makes sure that those who dedicated their lives to a cause do not go unnoticed or are not forgotten. Everyone has people in their life who uplift them, who guide them, and who make it easier to move forward. Be sure those people know the impact they have had.

The truth is, the legal community would look very different without the work of Ginsburg and O'Connor, and all those who came before them. They also inspired women outside of the legal field to pursue careers in fields that were previously dominated by men. The more we talk about their accomplishments, the more likely it is that other people will be inspired to follow suit.

Generations of women have been inspired to pursue careers because of women who paved the way. Ginsburg is one of those women.

"I probably wouldn't have gone to law school if O'Connor and Ginsburg hadn't blazed the trail," said Lithwick, "and I think that they laid down markers of how to achieve and how to keep pushing forward."

PART III

How to Be Brave and Create Change

"In my long life, I have seen great changes."
—*Ruth Bader Ginsburg in an essay published by the* New York Times.[1]

6

On Hardship

WHEN RUTH BADER GINSBURG WAS young, she was brought to tears when a teacher tried to make her write with her right hand even though she was naturally left-handed. She received a D in penmanship, she has frequently recounted, which resulted in the decision to never again write with her right hand, or receive another D.[1] As she got older, Ruth was forced to take home economics and cooking in preparation for becoming a housewife, and from a young age she envied the boys, because she would rather be in shop than learning how to cook or sew.[2]

Ginsburg was born a few years into the Great Depression and five years before World War II began. She was only eight years old when tragedy struck at Pearl Harbor. Her parents tried to protect their young Jewish daughter from photographs of death camps and the horrors of World War II, and though she has mostly happy memories of her Brooklyn neighborhood, Ginsburg has discussed how she became increasingly aware of anti-Semitic feelings coming from some neighbors and other US citizens. Soon after Pearl Harbor, Ginsburg's beloved cousin Seymour was inducted into the Army and ultimately served in Europe and the Pacific. Her childhood continued with the addition of frequent air raid drills and ration coupons. She and her classmates created a "victory garden" and filled it with vegetables.[3]

Unfortunately for Ginsburg, these hard times she faced as a young girl were just the preface to a life filled with hardship and plagued by multiple bouts of cancer that afflicted both those she loved and the justice herself.

It is weird to try to find lessons or meaning out of someone's hardship, and I don't necessarily want to dig deeply to try to prove a point. Instead, I will say that Ginsburg has overcome more than most should ever face, and that it is clear she finds support through her friends and family during hard times. Through it all—the obstacles placed in front of her due to her sex, the cancer she has fought, the losses she's suffered—Justice Ginsburg has used her work as a coping mechanism. She holds tightly to the idea that her work now can better the world for others as the light at the end of a long tunnel.

★ ★ ★

When Ruth was in high school, her beloved mother, Celia, was diagnosed with cervical cancer and did not live to see her daughter graduate. During an interview with NPR in 2019, Nina Totenberg said that to really know Ruth Bader Ginsburg is to understand that she is a "woman of unbelievable steel."

"She always looks for a way to do something," Totenberg said. "So, she'll say, well, no, taking care of a child just made me better able to study until four o'clock in the morning and then get up at seven and et cetera, et cetera. So you have to—you get an idea of her determination and steeliness."[4]

This resolve was instilled in her at an early age by her mother. Celia had always encouraged Ruth to be "independent and self-sufficient"[5] and she reiterated to her daughter two very important lessons. The first was "be a lady." This meant Ruth should always conduct herself civilly and not allow anger or envy to overcome her. The second lesson was to "be independent." This was a highly unusual lesson for a mother of the time to be teaching her young daughter, but Ruth took it to heart.[6]

Besides this important advice, Celia was a caring and supportive mother, who used to read Eleanor Roosevelt's "My Day" newspaper columns aloud to Ruth and taught her daughter about her Jewish heritage. She also enrolled Ruth in Hebrew school.[7] Ruth's life was very much shaped by her mother's love and goals for her daughter. Later in life, Ruth would wear one of her mother's pins on her suit lapel when she was doing something she thought her mom would be proud of.[8] Celia made sure to introduce Ruth to strong Jewish American women so Ruth had positive role models to look up to.[9]

"[Ginsburg was] formed by growing up with her mother and her mother's very deliberate ideas and hoping that her daughter would be able to be independent and actually work for a living," said Totenberg in a phone interview.

Celia's cancer had already spread by the time she was diagnosed. Ruth, who went by "Kiki" in her early years,[10] didn't tell anyone at school, and instead threw herself into her academics and extracurriculars during this time, earning top grades and a spot on the honor roll. She played cello in the orchestra and joined the student government, on top of participating in the booster club and being a baton twirler.[11]

Author Jane De Hart explained to me that Celia, even when very ill, emphasized that Ruth should carry on her life as normally as possible. She also made it very clear before she died that Ruth was expected to go to college.

"I think Ruth had a very clear idea of what her mother expected of her after her death," De Hart said.

Ruth once said her mother was "the strongest and bravest person" she's ever known.[12] After her death, Celia was buried next to her firstborn daughter, who had died from meningitis when Ruth was fourteen months old.[13]

Ruth went on to Cornell, where she met Marty. The couple fell in love and were married. Then devastation struck when Marty got word that he had testicular cancer while the two were students at Harvard. Though he was told his chances were extremely low, he fought a tough battle, with Ruth by his side. He survived, against all odds, and graduated.

Meanwhile, Ruth became one of the two women on the *Harvard Law Review* and was constantly reminded that she didn't belong in the men's club. There wasn't even a female bathroom in the main building where students took their exams.[14]

"You felt in class as if all eyes were on you and that if you didn't perform well, you would be failing not only for yourself, but for all women," Ginsburg said of her time at Harvard.[15]

Even though Marty was cancer-free, they were still unsure how long he would live, so when he got a job in New York, Ruth wanted to move with him. Except Dean Griswold wouldn't let her finish her Harvard degree at Columbia. So Ruth just transferred fully to Columbia—her reputation preceding her.

Then came the struggle to find a job (though Judge Palmieri later said that Ginsburg was one of his best clerks ever).[16] That clerkship opened doors for Ginsburg, and she finally received offers from a few corporate law firms— but luckily, Ginsburg instead went another direction. She accepted an offer to coauthor a book about civil procedure in Sweden, Marty agreed to hold the home front with Jane, and Ruth's first introduction to gender equality arrived. There is no silver lining or lesson to Ginsburg getting turned down by man after man for just being a woman, but it is clear that her life's trajectory—and the trajectory of women's equality under the law—might have been very different if she had settled in corporate law.

"So often in life, things that you regard as an impediment turn out to be a great good fortune," Ginsburg has said of not going into the corporate world.[17]

Ginsburg dove headfirst into litigating gender discrimination cases in the 1970s. Out of six cases argued before the Supreme Court, she won five. She was constantly readjusting her plan, keeping the endgame in sight.

It took her a while, and she was passed over multiple times,[18] but Ginsburg was finally nominated to the DC Circuit, where she continued to face discrimination (for example, when she and Marty would attend cocktail parties and the host would introduce "Judge Ginsburg," most people assumed that meant Marty and would hold out their hands to him). She solidified her image as a moderate judge, which ultimately led to intense criticism during her campaign for a

Supreme Court nomination. Despite the fact that President Bill Clinton initially believed women were against her (she was also seen as too old, since she was sixty), Ginsburg was nominated thanks to a campaign led valiantly by her husband and other women who went to bat for the fierce lawyer and judge. She then won over the Senate and ultimately, only three senators voted against her nomination to the court.[19] Once more, she was forced to deal with bathroom issues. In fact, it wasn't until Ginsburg joined the court that a women's bathroom was added, a sign, Ginsburg said, that "women were there to stay."[20]

Cancer reared its ugly head again and again. In September 1999, Ruth went to the doctor for an abdominal infection, and it was discovered that she had colon cancer. She had surgery and went through "precautionary" chemotherapy and radiation treatments.[21] In 2000, she said that she would only require "routine examinations to assure"[22] her continued good health. It was during one of the routine exams about ten years later that doctors found a single lesion in Ginsburg's pancreas. She underwent surgery that removed part of her pancreas and spleen.

Ginsburg scheduled treatment for both of these cancers during the court's off days. She did not miss a single day of oral argument.[23]

I want to take a moment to say that the key here is not to imitate Ginsburg's exact coping mechanisms—it is to find our own as we move throughout the world. There is of course no "right" response to grief or hardship. What worked for Ginsburg—immediately returning to work following tragedy and major surgery—might not work for you, and that's okay.

But what we can take away is that she has found ways to persevere again and again after difficult times in her life. For you, self-care or coping during hardship may look like getting back to work, or it may look like surrounding yourself with friends, making a meal once a week that honors someone you lost, turning your phone off, going to therapy, or allowing yourself to just be home, or all or none of the above. Whatever it is, do your best to find something that allows you to carry on in the healthiest way possible.

★ ★ ★

In 2005, Justice O'Connor announced she was leaving the court, an event followed quickly by Chief Rehnquist's death. It was the end of an era—the court had not changed in eleven years, and the nine justices had built "a sense of family."[24] Nearly two years after Rehnquist's death and O'Connor's departure, Ginsburg still felt deeply sad.[25]

And the court did change. President George Bush nominated Judge John Roberts to be the new chief justice and Judge Samuel Alito to be a new justice. At the same time Marty was diagnosed with cancer again, seven years after Ruth had pancreatic cancer surgery. As the Roberts court got underway, abortion came back on the docket, with *Gonzalez v. Carhart* fulfilling Ginsburg's fear that the shift in the court would challenge *Roe v. Wade*. Ginsburg dissented from the bench after the 5–4 decision was made, saying the decision was "alarming" and that it "tolerates, indeed applauds, federal intervention to ban nationwide a procedure found necessary and proper in certain cases."[26] Ginsburg concluded, saying that the Act could only be understood as an effort to chip away a right that had already been declared again and again by the court.[27]

That summer, Ginsburg added more speaking engagements to her agenda in order to try to get young women to care more about their reproductive rights and not take them for granted.[28]

She continued to dissent as the lonely years of her being the only woman on the court continued. Even Barack Obama winning the presidential election couldn't stop her from feeling Justice Sandra Day O'Connor's absence, as the men she sat beside consistently failed to understand what it was like to grow up as a woman in America.

To make matters nearly unbearable, Marty had only gotten worse. Then, Ginsburg herself was diagnosed with cancer at a very early stage. She had to undergo the removal of pancreatic cancer and get radiation and chemotherapy.[29] The Ginsburgs were fighting "cancer on two fronts," leaving the justice "exhausted and her formidable resolve depleted."[30] Author Jane De Hart writes in her biography of RBG that after her own diagnosis of pancreatic cancer, Ruth said to herself, "I will live. Not I hope I will live, but *I will live*."[31]

Though things briefly started to look up when President Obama nominated two women to the court, Sonia Sotomayor and Elena Kagan (though Ginsburg told Obama she would be even happier if he would give her four more),[32] it did not last long. Marty passed away from complications from cancer in 2010, within a week of their wedding anniversary.[33]

With the encouragement of her children, Ginsburg, "ashen-faced,"[34] appeared on the bench the next day.

Daughter Jane Ginsburg, according to the authors of *The Notorious RBG,* said that her father would not have wanted his wife to miss the last days of the term on account of his death.[35]

RBG spent the next few months carrying out all of her speaking engagements, but also participating in Marty's as well. Her daughter helped fill her fridge so that she wouldn't survive on "Jell-O and cottage cheese."[36] James Ginsburg was married the day after Marty's memorial service on September 3. His mother officiated.[37] RBG threw herself into her job, keeping her days highly structured and stepping up her social calendar in lieu of being able to rely on Marty's outgoing personality.[38] She continued dissenting and was no longer willing to compromise as she watched the court move further away from the goals she had fought so hard for as a litigator in the 1970s. These dissents elevated her to the social icon we now know her as.

Nonetheless, the hardships never slowed. Ginsburg needed a stent put in her heart in November 2014, though she made it back on the bench to hear oral arguments just five days later.[39] In 2016, her beloved friend Justice Antonin Scalia was found dead at a hunting lodge in West Texas. Ginsburg said the court would be a "paler place" without Scalia's stories and wit.[40] Though President Obama chose Judge Merrick Garland to take the conservative justice's place on the bench, the move was blocked by Mitch McConnell, the Republican majority leader of the Senate. Within just an hour of hearing Scalia had died, McConnell announced that the Senate would refuse to hold hearings because there was a presidential election in nine months.[41] The block was successful.

During the 2016 presidential election, the now more outspoken Justice Ginsburg criticized Republican nominee Donald Trump (perhaps because she didn't have Marty to offer prior feedback[42]), saying she "[couldn't] imagine what the country would be like"[43] if he were elected. Her fans and members of the legal world were stunned and horrified by her break with tradition. Trump fired back, calling the justice "a disgrace to the Court," and said her "mind was shot" and said she should resign.[44] The justice later walked back her comments. A few months later, to the shock of much of the world including Ginsburg, Trump won the presidential election.

The Republican Senate allowed the new president to fill Scalia's vacant seat with Neil Gorsuch. Then, Justice Anthony Kennedy, who had proved to be a surprising swing vote in recent years, retired, and President Trump nominated Brett Kavanaugh. After his nomination, Kavanaugh was accused of sexual assault by three women. He was eventually confirmed, following a hearing in front of the Senate Judiciary Committee (which was Republican-controlled at the time).[45] With these two confirmations, Ginsburg remains outnumbered by conservatives for the foreseeable future and fights an increasingly lonely battle from the bench, as one source put it to me.

Then, to the horror of her fans everywhere, Ginsburg fell in her office and broke three ribs in 2018. To yet again make matters worse, during the scans to look at the damage, doctors discovered lesions on her lungs. She had cancer surgery toward the end of the year.[46]

Though she did miss arguments during her recovery, on her first day back on the bench after her surgery, Ginsburg was the first justice to ask a question.[47]

★ ★ ★

"I have only the most pablum thing to say, which is that if RBG can work the way she has through colon cancer, pancreatic cancer, lung cancer, cracked ribs, and the loss of her darling Marty, then we are all wimps if we don't keep at it too," said former clerk Heather Elliott during an email interview.

Throughout much of these hardships, Ginsburg has been in the public eye, facing criticism from those who want her to retire and listening to conspiracy theories about how she is, in fact, dead.[48] Yet she continues to show up, to work, and to exercise. Just a few weeks after she had that stent placed in November 2014, Ginsburg hosted the creators of the Notorious RBG Tumblr in her chambers. During this visit, Ginsburg was asked what she wants to say to the young people who admire her in the wake of her surgery. "You can tell them," she responded, "I'll be back doing push-ups next week."[49]

She also continues to think about others. Just a few hours after her lung surgery in 2018, Ginsburg was calling journalist friends from her hospital bed, apologizing for not disclosing her illness, but saying she didn't want them to be "caught between [their] friendship with [her] and [their] professional obligation." Even at the worst times, she is more considerate than most.

Maybe it is because she has been through much more than any person should have to bear that she is able to be such a good support system to others in need. She has seen the best of times and the worst of times, and she's still here.

"You can't have it all, all at once," Ginsburg said during an interview with Katie Couric in 2014. "Who—man or woman—has it all, all at once? Over my lifespan I think I have had it all. But in different periods of time, things were rough."[50]

Totenberg, who has known and reported on Ginsburg for about fifty years, told me that during a "really terrible time" in her life, Ginsburg gave Totenberg the "best piece of advice anybody ever gave" her.

Totenberg's first husband was in the hospital and was undergoing major surgery. Totenberg was "all but glued to his bedside," but at a certain point, Ginsburg told Totenberg that she needed to make a change. At the core of it, Ginsburg's message was that, in order to survive, Totenberg needed to go home and go back to work.

"She said essentially, this is not a direct quote, you're not going to survive and you're not going to be doing him any good just hanging around the hospital," Totenberg told me. "And he will be coming home and you're going to need your strength and your ability and your welcoming ability for him when he gets home. And if you spend it all now, you won't have anything left. You need to stay who you are so you can be yourself for him. The person he loves for him."

Totenberg went back to work and "felt much better." She didn't turn in her best work, but she "did okay." And when her husband did come home, she felt "much more able to cope with the challenges" they still faced.

★ ★ ★

In hard times, Ginsburg remains passionate about the law, and always returns to the fight that has been a part of her whole life. After she had major surgery for pancreatic cancer in

2009, she attended a joint session with Congress. She didn't want anyone to think that the Supreme Court was all male.[51]

"I think her personal example of just fortitude and courage through all the adversity she's faced, both professional and personal, is very inspiring and makes you want to work harder as well," said Associate Justice of the California Supreme Court Goodwin Liu, a former clerk.

Again, none of this is to say you should immediately return to work after a hard time. Everyone copes and grieves in different ways. Instead, find what is best for you. It may take a while and it may take adjustments, but you can follow Ginsburg's example of utilizing mechanisms and a schedule that works as well as possible for her.

Paul Schiff Berman, another one of Ginsburg's former clerks, said that the justice always remembers what is important to her and even in tough times, works toward those goals.

"Ginsburg is very quiet of course, but she has a steely and ferocious tenacity, and she keeps her eyes on what matters to her: the law and getting it right and making the world a more just place," said Berman. She focuses on doing the "best work" she can for others right now.

Another note is that Ginsburg has made adjustments following these hardships. Marty was always the life of the party, while Ruth was usually standing away from the crowd.[52] After his death, she had to come out of her shell, even just a little. She began to get more candid about her life and she started to be interviewed more.

"I think actually interestingly after [Marty] passed away, which was obviously a big loss for her, she came out of her shell a little bit," said Justice Liu. "She didn't have Marty to do all the ice-breaking social work for her, and she has managed her public persona in a really effective way."

Judge Robert Katzmann, who helped Ginsburg when she was working toward the Supreme Court, put it well in the chapter he wrote of *The Legacy of Ruth Bader Ginsburg*. He writes that RBG is determined to meet even the most difficult of personal and professional challenges, to struggle through all obstacles put in front of her, if it means helping guarantee a better future for both those who are here today and for those who will follow behind.[52]

Journalist Marvin Kalb echoed that sentiment when I asked him about what we can learn from Ginsburg's career and the hardships she faced. He thinks that Ginsburg would say to never give up, never stop fighting for what you believe in. She made it through hardship, but she also kept working to make it better for those who came after her. Because, at the end of the day, she wants to make the world better.

"Nine out of ten other women, faced with the kind of medical problems that she has, would've given up by now. Would've moved down to Florida to sit at the beach. But not her," Kalb said with a slight chuckle. "She feels that while she still has energy and her mind is still very sharp, she's going to continue the battle. Because it has not yet been won. And the idea is that you don't give up, you keep fighting for what you believe in."

At the end of the day, you know what is best for you and your own well-being. Follow RBG's path and do just that.

*Since this book was written, it was announced Justice Ginsburg had been treated for pancreatic cancer in August 2019. Following the news, the Supreme Court announced that no further treatment was needed at the time. Post treatment, RBG continued to travel and make public appearances.

7

On Persuasion over Anger

SHE NEVER THOUGHT IT WOULD happen. After having her "good job" for more than a decade, Justice Ruth Bader Ginsburg was surrounded by men every time she took her seat on the highest bench in the land. By the time 2009 rolled around, Justice Sandra Day O'Connor had been retired for a few years and RBG was beginning to feel the strain of being the sole female justice on the Supreme Court.

Though she had started to "find her voice"[1] through dissenting starting around 2007, Ginsburg had continued to remain cordial and collegial on the bench. But things hit a breaking point for the justice on April 21, 2009. That day, the Supreme Court heard arguments in the case, *Safford Unified School District v. Redding,* in which a thirteen-year-old girl was forced to strip down because of an anonymous tip that had led the school administration to believe the young girl, Savana Redding, was selling drugs.[2] During the trial, Redding called it the "most humiliating experience I have ever had. I held my head down so they could not see I was about to cry."[3] The young girl, who was a self-described nerd and an honor student, developed stomach ulcers following the event and eventually transferred to a different school.[4] Her mother sued the school under the claim that her daughter's constitutional rights had been violated.

However, the male justices of the Supreme Court did not seem to think the situation sounded that much different from having to change in front of people for gym class. The case seemed kind of "giggly" to them. They were clueless to what young girls' lives were like, having never been young girls themselves, and their responses made it clear they did not think what happened was a huge deal, since people change clothes for gym all the time.

"I'm trying to work out why this is a major thing to, say, strip down to your underclothes, which children do when they change for gym. . . . How bad is this?" questioned Justice Stephen Breyer.[5]

Ginsburg, on the other hand, found nothing funny about the strip search and looked like she "might explode,"[6] Nina Totenberg wrote. The only female justice on the bench "bristled, her eyes flashing with anger,"[7] to point out that Redding had to "shake [her] bra out, shake, [and stretch] the top of her underpants" on top of the fact that she was required to sit outside the vice principal's office for two hours. This put the teenager in a "humiliating position."[8] According to Totenberg, Ginsburg's voice "dripp[ed] with exasperation."[9] In an article written following the hearing, Totenberg wrote that "Ginsburg seemed to all but shout, boys may like to preen in the locker room, but girls, particularly teenage girls, do not."[10]

Ginsburg's anger did not seem to impact Justice Breyer's thoughts, as he continued, saying, "In my experience when I was 8 or 10 or 12 years old, you know, we *did* take our clothes off once a day, we changed for gym, OK? In my experience, too, people did sometimes stick things in my underwear."[11] When the spectators giggled at that, Breyer quickly tried to clarify, saying, "Or not *my* underwear. Whatever. Whatever. I was the one who did it? I don't know. I mean, I don't think it's beyond human experience."[12]

Dahlia Lithwick told me that the Redding case was the "closest" she ever saw to Ginsburg "losing it on the bench." Those emotions the justice felt clearly did not dissipate. In an unprecedented move, Ginsburg herself gave an interview to *USA Today*'s Joan Biskupic while the *Redding* decision was still pending.

"They have never been a 13-year-old girl. . . . It's a very sensitive age for a girl. I didn't think my colleagues, some of them, quite understood," she said during the interview. She then made the case for why the court desperately needed another female justice. "The differences between male and female justices are . . . seldom in the outcome." She then paused, before continuing: "It is sometimes in the outcome."[13]

She continued to give interviews that summer, saying that her male colleagues had not tried to imagine what the situation was like for a thirteen-year-old girl. "I think many of [the male justices] first thought of their own reaction. It came out in various questions: You change your clothes in the gym, what's the big deal?"[14] She emphasized the need for more women on the bench, saying that the image of a single woman on the bench will confuse younger generations who come to visit the court. "Young women are going to think, *Can I really aspire to that kind of post?*"[15]

It seemed as if something had "finally snapped" in the only remaining female justice. A lifetime worth of laughing along with, or ignoring the laughter of, her male colleagues had caught up with her, writes Lithwick in *The Legacy of Ruth Bader Ginsburg*.[16] The time had come for Ginsburg to stop "choking down"[17] her outrage. She had spent her whole life avoiding making waves. But that desire was waning.[18]

★ ★ ★

The pure fact that Ginsburg had, for the first time, shown real anger on the bench sixteen years after she took the Supreme Court Oath, is a great example of both who she is and what she believes. Ginsburg does not lose her temper. She remains scholarly and cordial and, instead of trying to use anger to sway her opponents, she attempts to persuade. Her attitude toward anger provides an important lesson. While anger sometimes has a place in this world, it is worth trying to persuade someone to join your line of thought through cold hard facts and a strong argument.

In an op-ed for the *New York Times* about how to live a good life, Ginsburg urges people to "fight for the things you care about but do it in a way that will lead others to join you."[19]

It's great advice, of course, but incredibly hard to carry out.

"I think it's not easy to do what she does about not losing her temper or not getting angry," Totenberg told me with a laugh during our interview.

Ginsburg originally learned this lesson from something her mother used to repeat, former clerk Paul Schiff Berman explained.

"She's talked often about her mother's advice 'to be a lady,' and what she took from that was to be her own person and not get buffeted or thrown off stride by anger or disillusionment or petty jealousies," he said during a phone interview.

So she didn't. Her method of fighting is with words and almost everything she does harkens back to the idea that we can still persuade others to see it our way. As a litigator, RBG won five of the six antidiscrimination cases she argued before the Supreme Court in the 1970s because of "logic, not fireworks."[20]

"Don't take no for an answer," Ginsburg said during an interview in 2012. "But also, don't react in anger . . . Regard every encounter as an opportunity to teach someone."[21]

This advice also just shows how women conducted themselves during the time period that Ginsburg was raised. She was given the identity of a feminist firebrand. But, Lithwick writes in *The Legacy of Ruth Bader Ginsburg,* she is "both by choice and necessity, a firebrand made of ice," like most women who grew up in the 1950s.[22]

She was raised in a time period where women had to hold all emotions in.[23] After the *Redding* case, Ginsburg told Joan Biskupic that she couldn't count how many meetings she went to in the 1960s and 1970s where she would say something that she considered to be a pretty good idea, and then "somebody would say exactly what [she] said. Then people would become alert to it [and] respond."[24] Ginsburg told Biskupic that this even happened while she was on the court—but much more frequently once O'Connor left—in which she would say something and it wasn't "until some-body else says it that everyone will focus on the point."[25] Still, Ginsburg remained so reserved that if you sat next to her at a dinner party you needed to either ask her about her "children or the law" in order to get her to talk.[26]

A friend of Ginsburg's, Cynthia Fuchs Epstein, once said the justice has achieved a lot through her "white glove" style, one that is very conscious of etiquette.[27]

Epstein's right; Ginsburg has seen success through this method. Because she has been forced to distill her anger for so long, Ginsburg long ago figured out the best ways to use it. Just like it sometimes pays to be a little deaf in your marriage (or on the court), it pays to keep your anger at bay until you get what you want.

"She stays in this realm of emotional and intellectual depth and doesn't get lured into superficial arguments or the seductive power of outrage," former clerk Elizabeth Porter explained to me.

For example, during our interview, Totenberg men-tioned the famous story of when Ginsburg was arguing a case in front of the Supreme Court when she was a lawyer. One of her colleagues asked her why she wasn't answering Justice Stevens (she had twice avoided answering his questions), and Ginsburg responded, "Because if I'd answered it, I might've lost Justice Powell's vote, and if I didn't answer Stevens, I was going to get his vote anyway."[28]

She is also not the only justice who held it all in for decades. Justice Sandra Day O'Connor was also raised during the same time and seemed to agree that anger won't win you battles. Both she and Ginsburg dealt with a lot in order to keep people close who would ultimately help them. In her book *Sisters in*

Law, lawyer and author Linda Hirsham tells two stories of odd friendships: one of O'Connor and one of Ginsburg, who both maintained pleasant relationships with men who were not doing much to advance women's rights.[29] Hirsham writes that it's possible they could only do this because both women held strongly to the idea that they were "natural members of the formerly all-male elite"[30] or perhaps it is just because they had grown up facing such discrimination that they saw no other way. Whatever the reason, O'Connor and Ginsburg both separately tuned out certain perspectives held by these men in order to accomplish a greater good down the road.

For O'Connor, this meant that even though she supported the Equal Rights Amendment, she kept up a lifelong friendship with conservative Barry Goldwater, who was an "early and vocal opponent" of the ERA. And for Ginsburg, this meant maintaining a friendly correspondence with "legendary antifeminist" University of Chicago law professor Philip Kurland.[31]

Hirsham explains that these connections ultimately paid off for both women. When antiabortion activists tried to keep O'Connor off the court in 1981, Goldwater was still powerful, and he used the power to speak up in support of O'Connor, saying anyone "who opposed her should be spanked." Years into their friendly back-and-forth, Ginsburg wanted Kurland to help her daughter, then a student at the University of Chicago. So Ginsburg politely wrote him a cute note, describing all of her daughter's strengths and explaining her merit, just like men in power have done for decades.[32]

★ ★ ★

The method of persuasion over anger has clearly not affected RBG's ability to make systematic changes to the law, as we can see through her historic legacy. None of this is to say that Ginsburg doesn't feel angry or have a limit. After all, she's human, and she's spent her life fighting against discrimination and sexism while actively facing it herself. However, she is able, as former clerk Berman put it, "to always find within herself a place of quiet resolve."

And holding her tongue, or seeing the power in persuasion and not anger, doesn't make her weak. For example, when Ginsburg was nominated to the Supreme Court in 1993, someone sent her a fax to let her know that the guys in law school used to call her by the nickname "Bitch." Ginsburg responded by saying, "Better bitch than mouse."[33] Lithwick explained to me that RBG has just always been "unbelievably cautious" about expressing her anger. Throughout everything she has faced—being asked why she was taking a man's place at Harvard, getting turned down for jobs because of her gender, getting called Justice O'Connor by lawyers who are arguing in front of the Supreme Court—Ginsburg has mostly been able to temper her anger. Lithwick wrote once that even when she was "absolutely maddened" by what the court had decided, she kept a cordial and collegial tone.[34]

Then things changed. For the first twelve and a half years on the court, Ginsburg had Justice O'Connor beside her. Even though they did not always agree on the final decisions, they both understood gender discrimination differently than their male counterparts, because they had personally experienced it. After O'Connor left, the court began to swing further and further to the right, and Ginsburg became unwilling to just sit back while her colleagues were diminishing or belittling real experiences of women, many of which she had personally experienced and been forced to play down in her own life.[35]

As she felt more and more lonely as the only woman on the court, RBG began to show the tension and anger she had been holding in all those years. She started speaking up more about her own experiences where she felt marginalized to try and finally repair existing injustices, but also to vocalize the "slights and slurs" she had previously been reluctant to speak about when she was a young lawyer. She was finally discussing the years in which she had been talking but no one was listening.[36]

So Ginsburg started dissenting, to the delight of feminists from the 1970s who remembered her well-written arguments and to the shock of those who sat beside her on the court. Again, her dissents have never just been a way to unload nearly eighty-six years of anger toward the way women and minorities are treated. Ginsburg's dissents still have one of two goals: either persuade Congress to do something and make a change where the court cannot; or address future generations.[37] She has been successful, sometimes. On the rare occasion, her dissents have caused Congress to write laws and have persuaded other justices to change their minds. Through all this, she has remained herself.[38]

Nonetheless, she still isn't yelling. RBG's sizzling dissents may strike a chord for many, but she's not screaming from the bench, and it is almost as if her dissents have become the next step in her carefully calculated plan. Every female in America who has been employed has likely experienced and therefore understands the systemic unfairness that permeates all work cultures. Ginsburg has worked her whole life to highlight these experiences and describe them in a way that her male colleagues might understand. But the time had come where she, as Lithwick, who has written on this exact topic multiple times, once put it, just "doesn't want to talk about it in polite whispers anymore."[39]

She is still working to persuade, and her endgame is still the same. Her tone may have changed, but she's still putting the institution first, she's still working with people she disagrees with, she's still ultimately fighting for the same thing she's been fighting for all along. Lithwick writes in *The Legacy of Ruth Bader Ginsburg* that RBG spent her life lodged between intellectualism and daily sexism. She built a "career of marrying the two."[40]

An important note is that by doing so, she gained the respect of her colleagues and the public. She has kept her head down and silently worked toward her goals. In direct opposition to the tale of the girl who cried wolf, Ginsburg speaking out against past and current injustices really means something. She is finally going to war.

"Her field of battle is the law," explained journalist Marvin Kalb to me. "And her arena is the Supreme Court. And she's got her army of passion, fact, determination . . . stubborn, a stubborn determination to do something good, for the social good."

★ ★ ★

Now, don't get me wrong: The lesson here is not "don't be angry" or "bottle it all in." There are, of course, plenty of things in this world to be mad about, and we shouldn't ignore them—Ginsburg certainly doesn't. Her dissents from the bench are part of the reason we think of her as a feminist firebrand at all (bolstered, of course, by her work in the 1970s), and there have been cases that produced that flash of anger in Ginsburg's eyes. But at the end of the day, she cares more about the outcome in Court than she does her own emotions, and she will put the institution first in order to try to see tangible changes in the law. Her dissents are still based in the idea that either the country or Congress will be persuaded to make change.

"I think part of it is that she has a laser focus on doing the best work she can do for the world now," said Berman, her former clerk.

All of this is to say that RBG, of course, like probably every woman in America, feels angry, perhaps now more than ever, as abortion cases threaten to make their way to the court and she is finding herself more frequently a part of the minority opinion than the majority. Thus, she has let emotion show now and again—like in 2016 with her comments on Trump.

For Justice Ginsburg, the point of talking about the injustices she faced was to further the ultimate goal of eradicating gender discrimination. That is why she has started to speak out more in the past decade—she has been forced to watch the court chip away at her life's work.

Ironically, her dissents have helped fuel the idea that it is okay to show your anger. "Women do now feel entitled to show anger and these angry dissents for that reason have fueled this iconic status (of Ginsburg)," said Joan Williams, a professor at UC Hastings College of the Law.

But Lithwick pointed out in *The Atlantic* that the "rule-abiding, institutionalist, cautious lawyer and then judge" in fact managed "to remake constitutional history precisely because of these qualities, not despite them."[41] This can be hard for some of her fans to reconcile.

During our interview, Lithwick explained that Ginsburg's ability to control her anger shows there is a benefit to working within the institution that you are in, and that is a lesson we should all pay attention to.

"Especially because I think we're going through a moment of really reifying women's anger right now, and I think that she offers this interesting counter narrative," Lithwick said. "Which is not to devalue women's anger—I think there is a huge place for just distilled rage—but I also think she is a trailblazer insofar that she is a lifelong institution actor . . . a lot of people that we think of as badasses are also lifelong institution actors, and there's real power in working within institutions."

Getting on board with this tempered anger, this decision to try to teach others the importance of seeing things differently, can be difficult for a generation of young women who are really sick and tired of teaching men. As Lithwick wrote in 2018, women no longer "believe that men who only see sexism when it affects their wives and daughters are genuinely fighting for equality."[42]

So where does that leave us? Is Ginsburg's strategy of empathy, compassion, and persuasion too old-fashioned? Is Ginsburg's history of gently teaching men, like a kindergarten teacher would, that women are important and visible, "disempowering"?[43]

The women of today march in the street, they are speaking out against sexual harassment and assault, they're finding their voice, and realizing that they can do whatever they want in this world. Feminists who love the Notorious RBG have to "reckon with this paradox," Lithwick once wrote.[44] The woman they hold in such high esteem for her stinging dissents still rarely raises her voice, and in fact, she got this far in life by "being the very opposite of a firebrand."[45] She is still a team player first, and still puts the institution ahead of anything else. Her ability to control her anger, like her friendship with Scalia, is sometimes hard for young feminists to stomach.

But Lithwick made an incredible point in an article on this very topic in *The Atlantic*. She writes that she "appreciated that steady Ginsburg—who has always toiled within the guardrails of the law and the Constitution—far more than the gangsta-feminist we've turned her into."[46] She goes on to say that the Ginsburg is a little bit of a dork, she's a perfectionist and an idealist who loves good writing and powerful music. And finally, Lithwick explains, Ginsburg believes "the pursuit of justice is a holy project seared into the DNA of her Jewish ancestors."[47]

And that's what we need to remember. Ginsburg walks slowly, she talks even more slowly, she thinks before she speaks, and she never forgets the goal that she has in mind. She uses her smarts and the facts to win cases and win people over. The Notorious RBG is an icon, and in no way should that be taken away from her. She has encouraged and inspired hundreds of thousands if not millions of people, and for good reason. She herself has long said that women in the generations below her need to step up and start fighting the fight that Ginsburg has been leading for decades. She wants us to follow her path. She needs us to fight back against the inequalities and injustices that seem to be popping up daily right now. What we need to remember, and what we should take away from her approach, is that it pays to be strategic about the way you show your anger.

"She doesn't allow herself to get thrown off balance by the moment-to-moment emotions that can be whipped up, and I think that's very hard in this day and age," said former clerk Berman. "There are so many things to be outraged about, and justifiably so, but it can throw you off-balance as an individual, and so you always have to think about who you are, center yourself, and think about what is important not just now but five, ten, fifteen years from now, what are the eternal things that are important and how do you move in those directions and not let yourself be buffeted by transient emotional whiplash."

The former clerk echoed the idea that in this day and age, it's hard not to get mad at everything happening in the world and it's easy to think that will never change. Maybe what we all need to do is look at Ginsburg's long history of strategically and pointedly making substantial changes to American law by being a reserved radical.

"One is tempted to think that persuasion is no longer possible because there is nobody left who can be persuaded of anything anymore, but she truly believes in the slow process of persuasion, and she has succeeded time and again in bringing people around to her positions," said Berman. "And if you believe in the value of law, at all—obviously some people don't, but if you do believe in the value of law—part of its value is the possibility of slow persuasion over time based on rational argument, because that's the legal process, that's how law evolves."

For Ginsburg, the end goal is and always has been to change the law. She lives by the observation spoken by Justice Benjamin Cardozo: "Justice is not to be taken by storm. She is to be wooed by slow advances."[48]

8

On Why, and How, to Dissent

In 1998, LILLY LEDBETTER LEARNED she had been making 40 percent less money than her male coworkers, all of whom worked the same position as her but a different shift, at the Goodyear Tire factory in Alabama. Though Ledbetter had started out with the same salary as the men at the factory, she was given lower raises over the years. She had been at the company for nineteen years when someone slipped her a note to alert her to the pay discrepancy.[1] She realized in that moment that her that her retirement, her 401(k), and her Social Security were all likely affected by this nearly two decades of underpayment while working at the dirty, smelly, and hot factory.[2]

In 1998, Ledbetter sued, claiming pay discrimination under Title VII of the Civil Rights Act of 1964 and the Equal Pay Act of 1963. The Supreme Court ruled that Ledbetter had filed her lawsuit too late. The majority did agree that

Ledbetter was a victim of pay discrimination but urged plaintiffs in cases like hers to "sue early on."[3]

Justice Ruth Bader Ginsburg didn't like this decision. In a rare move, she read a stinging dissent from the bench, saying, "The Court does not comprehend or is indifferent to the insidious way in which women can be victims of pay discrimination."[4]

In reading her dissent, Ginsburg hoped to elicit a reaction from another branch of government. Ginsburg wanted Congress or the president to immediately fix what the court could not.[5] RBG addressed the public through her dissent, trying to urge women to not allow the court majority to have the final word on the meaning of gender discrimination.

It worked. The Lilly Ledbetter Fair Pay Act was the first bill signed into law by President Barack Obama in 2009. It amends Title VII of the Civil Rights Act of 1964 by asserting that the statute of limitations for filing an equal-pay lawsuit regarding pay discrimination resets with each new paycheck affected by any discriminatory action.[6]

Ledbetter has said that personally, Ginsburg's dissent "meant the world"[7] to her and that she still gets chills and goosebumps just thinking about it.[8] Linda Greenhouse, the *New York Times* reporter, called Ledbetter after the dissent was read and told the plaintiff that Ginsburg's "words bounced off the wall, I wish you could've heard it."[9]

★ ★ ★

There is so much to learn from Ginsburg's dissents, but the biggest is to not remain silent in the face of injustice. The other is to know what type of dissent (or, in a nonlegal context, argument or statement) will work best for the situation.

There are two kinds of dissents in Ginsburg's mind. There is the dissent she used in the Ledbetter case, to urge Congress or the president to take immediate action. Another form of dissent speaks to a future age.[10] Ginsburg is ever hopeful that if the court has any blind spots, their eyes will be opened later down the road, because justices are always thinking and changing.[11]

"Although RBG would prefer to be in the majority, the ability to speak out in disagreement in the form of a dissenting opinion is incredibly important for the losing side, future litigants and judges, and most of all, to sound the alarm to the public," Shana Knizhnik, an attorney and coauthor of the book *Notorious RBG: The Life and Times of Ruth Bader Ginsburg*, once explained to NBC News.[12]

Though she was seen as "excessively liberal"[13] during her litigator years, Judge Ginsburg was actually known as a "consensus builder"[14] when she was on the DC Circuit Court and would have been the least likely person to seek out the type of limelight she has attained from her dissents. When Court decisions are announced from the bench, usually only the majority opinion is summarized. The separate opinions of any justice, either dissenting or concurring, are noted, but it is actually very rare for a dissent to be given from the bench. During her first twelve terms, Ginsburg only gave six dissents from the bench.[15] These oral dissents show, as Justice John Paul Stevens once said, that Ginsburg believes the court's opinion is not only wrong, but "profoundly misguided."[16] The oral dissent was never necessarily "Justice Ginsburg's style," wrote Linda Greenhouse.[17]

Then during the second term of the Roberts Court (which began in 2005), she found herself the most senior liberal member of a more conservative Court, Ginsburg "found her voice and used it," employing "passionate and pointed" words.[18] By the end of 2014, Ginsburg had delivered twelve bench dissents, becoming the court's most frequent bench dissenter.[19] She also gave more dissents in a single term (2012–2013) than any other justice in nearly three decades.[20]

"It's partially that [Ginsburg] began as the Court has gone further and further to the right, she began to be much more confrontative," said Joan Williams, a professor at UC Hastings College of the Law. "She concluded that she couldn't win. She was willing to compromise and work with people so long as she could win cases, but now there's no way in God's green Earth she's going to win so she's just going to say what she thinks."

Ginsburg's role changed, Williams explained to me, and when the justice realized she wasn't going to win cases, she became a "speaking-truth-to-power person." This is also how Ginsburg tells the story.

"I don't think I changed. Perhaps I am a little less tentative than I was when I was a new justice," she said during an interview in 2014. "But what really changed was the composition of the Court."[21]

★ ★ ★

Her goal was never to become notorious. It wasn't until 2013, when the court majority struck down a section of the Voting Rights Act—which prohibited districts from enacting changes to their election law and procedures without getting official approval first—that the dissents really started flowing. The Act had originally been created in 1965 in response to the country's history of voting discrimination.

It was a 5–4 decision in the case of *Shelby County v. Holder*, with Ginsburg on the losing side. Ginsburg wrote a blistering defense, which asserted, among other things, that throwing out this preclearance because it was working was like "throwing away your umbrella in a rainstorm because you're not getting wet."[22] Reading from the bench, she quoted Martin Luther King Jr., "The arc of the moral universe is long, but it bends towards justice," before adding her final statement: "if there is a steadfast commitment to see the task through to completion. That commitment has been disserved by today's decision."[23]

And the Notorious RBG was born. Shana Knizhnik, at the time a New York University Law School student, created a Tumblr page with the name after she saw her friend hashtag it, in the hopes of it "(doing) something positive" in light of the upsetting Court decision.[24] She posted Ginsburg's dissent. Then, the name took off, and as Ginsburg's reputation as a dissenter grew, the name spread, spawning T-shirts (which RBG now gives as gifts[25]), candles, mugs, and more. You can buy bobbleheads or pins with the image of Ginsburg wearing a crown. There's even a song written about her dissent in *Burwell v. Hobby Lobby*. If you want, you can buy merch that shows Ginsburg holding up two middle fingers (heads up: it is definitely photoshopped). You can even purchase Halloween costumes or just a dissent collar, which Ginsburg wears when she is in the minority opinion.

★ ★ ★

Part of the reason RBG became so notorious and so respected for her opinions is something we discussed in the last chapter: she spent most of her life playing by the rules. This is not an easy thing to do, but it meant she gained a lot of respect. When she started speaking up, people listened intently, and though the Lilly Ledbetter Fair Pay Act of 2009 is one of the few times there was an actual change, her speaking up did, and does, have an impact.

Since she started reading her dissents, she has never apologized for doing so. "I will continue to give voice to my dissent if, in my judgment, the court veers in the wrong direction when important matters are at stake," she said at the end of 2007 term.[26] Here's the thing: Ginsburg isn't dissenting because she likes it but instead because she sees the act as a part of her democratic responsibility.[27]

"When a justice is of the firm view that the majority got it wrong, she is free to say so in dissent. I take advantage of that prerogative, when I think it important, as do my colleagues," Ginsburg wrote in a *New York Times* opinion piece.[28]

RBG's dissents find the intersection between legal arguments and human implications of the court's decisions.[29] They are also what has made her pop-culture icon status skyrocket, despite her age and quiet demeanor and the fact that a majority of Americans probably couldn't tell you the names of even three Supreme Court justices (though Thurgood Marshall did also become a household name during his time on the court). Dahlia Lithwick once wrote in *Slate* that on and off the bench, "Ginsburg always looked and sounded like the most dangerous weapon she could possibly be carrying would be a potato kugel."[30]

Now due to her powerhouse dissents, she has come to be seen as a badass. Following her dissent in *Shelby County*, she fired off heated opinions in the Texas affirmative action case *Fisher v. University of Texas*. Then the real rock-star status hit after her dissent in *Burwell v. Hobby Lobby*, in which she spoke vehemently for women's reproductive rights and said she feared the court had "walked into a minefield."[31] That's really when the memes and tribute songs kicked off.

Her dissents, and the mania surrounding them, were also a part of a sudden and unexpected celebration of the power of the older, and mostly "politically authoritative women"[32] by a "democratized, raucous communicative organ that is the Internet, in which a diverse rabble of young people make their own messages," pointed out journalist Rebecca Traister in the *New Republic*.[33]

They are also a reminder that even if you are on the losing side, you can still have the last word. And that last word just might start a revolution. So if you find yourself in a losing battle, it is important to remember how to dissent like RBG.

★ ★ ★

A big lesson from Notorious RBG's dissents goes right back to the idea that anger is not necessarily in Ginsburg's play-book. Even when she dissents, she doesn't speak angrily, but instead acknowledges her opponent's side before discussing her opinion. She never patronizes her colleagues or their ideas (there's that collegiality idea again). She also does not want to risk losing the public's faith in the judiciary system or process by insulting her colleagues. Ginsburg has said that the most effective dissent, in her mind, is one that can survive purely on its own legal basis.[34]

There is an important lesson here in remembering that belittling your opponent does nothing to further your argument and will likely make them less interested in listening anyway. But the even bigger lesson we should all learn from Justice Ginsburg is this: words have impact, and they matter, therefore you have to take them seriously. Every. Single. One.

"She was borderline obsessive about getting the words right," said David Post, who clerked for Ginsburg when she was a judge in DC and then again when she was on the Supreme Court.

Post remembered when he was clerking for her on the DC Appeals Court and they were discussing a draft he had written.

"I had used some word in the draft like, 'The defendant claimed' . . . or something, and we were talking about it and she said, 'You don't really say the defendants claimed, the plaintiffs claim but defendants don't claim, should it be asserted or averred or stated or observed or," Post said. "We went through this thing and I remember thinking at the time, 'Oh God, if she does this for every word it's going to take forever.'"

Ginsburg's focus on the importance of words dates all the way back to her Cornell days. It was there her European literature professor, Vladimir Nabokov, taught her the importance of both picking the right words and organizing them correctly.

It is also vital to remember that change does not come swiftly, no matter how powerful your pen is. More often than not, our dissenting opinions will not change things immediately. Just like Ginsburg's strategy when she was a litigator, her dissents keep her eyes on the prize. In that vein, you want to make everything you write and say is building toward that goal.

"She plays the long and slow game," Post said. "She's a very methodical person, makes her a good judge I think, 'cause she thinks that way, and she writes that way, this paragraph leads to this paragraph leads to this paragraph all the way to the end till you're done, step-step-step-step-step till the conclusion."

Ginsburg also does not dissent every single time she disagrees. Reading an oral dissent from the bench is a big deal, and doing so frequently would lessen the impact that they have. Ginsburg is extremely pragmatic and strategic in choosing her battles—we've seen that in the way she worked as a litigator in the 1970s all the way to her time on the court.

"She has not hesitated to be outspoken if she thought her dissent was right and had a realistic chance of becoming a winning position in the near future, so I think she has picked her political battles pretty wisely," said Scott Dodson, editor of *The Legacy of Ruth Bader Ginsburg*.

It can be easy to get up in arms about everything that feels unfair or unequal in our society, but we all, like Ginsburg, should choose to dissent at the times where it will truly land well and be heard.

"I try to follow Justice Brandeis' counsel," Ginsburg once said about dissenting during a speech. "He cautioned that in most matters of statutory interpretation, 'it is more important

that [the applicable] rule of law be settled than that it be settled right.'"[35]

★ ★ ★

Before she dissents, RBG asks herself if it is really necessary.[36]
If there are multiple dissenters for one case, Ginsburg would
also prefer that they all agree to take the same course, because
one opinion speaks louder than four. She has stated that in the
rush to judge *Bush v. Gore* (2000), the press and public had to
read four pretty long dissents because there wasn't time to just
compose one. This meant that the nation was left to their own
devices to discern what each justice felt.[37]

The justice has also seen dissents as a conversation among
justices and believes that dissents help the writer of the majority
opinion firm up their thoughts—and that this is a good thing,
allowing for a better opinion overall from the court. She said
that "more often than not, my colleagues' comments help me
improve an opinion." And though she will try her hardest to
get it right and keep it tight, the discussion among justices is
helpful.[38] The best way to do it is circulate the opinion to both
justices in the majority and minority, see what they say, then
refine and clarify.[39]

During a Reuters interview in 2012, Ginsburg said, "It
ain't over 'til it's over," and mentioned that justices do shift
positions as they work on cases and read each other's draft
opinions.

"People change their minds about what they thought,"
Ginsburg said. "So it isn't at all something extraordinary, and
that's how it should work. We're in the process of trying to
persuade each other and then the public."[40]

What can we take from that idea? That if you are arguing with or if you disagree with someone, listen, truly listen, to their side. It might help bolster your own argument. But in strengthening your own argument by listening and responding to critiques, you might also help sway your opponent's mind. Ginsburg has once written a dissent for herself and one other justice. But over time, it became the opinion of the court from which only three other justices dissented.

From that moment on, any time she dissents, Ginsburg aims for a repeat of that experience. It has only gotten rarer that a majority member will turn, but RBG is ever the optimist.[41]

★ ★ ★

Though Ginsburg would prefer not to dissent so much, she has no plans to compromise just to put on a united front.

NPR's Nina Totenberg said to me on the phone that though she has not discussed this directly with the justice, she thinks Ginsburg is "less willing to compromise now, except if she can get an opinion."

Ginsburg herself has said that though she appreciates "the value of unanimous opinions," she will "continue to speak in dissent when important matters are at stake."[42] We can all learn from this, and make it a practice ourselves to speak up loudly in the face of adversity. However, it is more than that. Before we all go forth and loudly dissent, it is worth remembering dissents are also about picking your battles, choosing your words carefully, speaking tactfully and without insult, and learning when your words will have the most impact.

9
On Creating Change and a Legacy

To some, she will be remembered as a judge. To others, a justice. Some people will think of her as the badass Notorious RBG, while there will be a few who only recognize her face from memes they've seen online. Her ACLU colleagues might remember her as a feminist litigator while members of the public will thank her for her dissents. Law students will credit her with why they chose their career. I'll always remember her as a female icon who taught me words can create change.

To her granddaughter, she'll always be Bubbie.[1]

RBG isn't planning on going anywhere right now, but her legacy is already enshrined in history.

Ruth Bader Ginsburg once wrote that she wants to be someone who is always willing to learn and listen, someone who is an independent thinker but who does not have a drafty mind.[2] However, it's pretty clear that if you've made it to this chapter of the book, you agree with me that RBG is not giving herself nearly enough credit.

"Many young people want to change the world. RBG did that," said Professor Stephanie Wildman, coeditor of the book *Women and the Law*, to me. "She inspires us, and she makes us hopeful about the good in society and in ourselves. Fighting against great odds, she prevailed and now has become an honored figure."

RBG's legacy started even before she became a Supreme Court justice. She fundamentally changed the way women and men legally exist in the United States when she worked as a litigator. Ginsburg famously believes that "Only when fathers are equal parents to their children will women truly be free,"[3] and she spent her life, slowly, steadily, methodically working toward that utopian world.

President Bill Clinton recognized these efforts in his speech in the White House Rose Garden after he nominated Ginsburg to the court. He first spoke of her legal background, the obstacles she faced and overcame, and her character. He then highlighted her repeated efforts to improve the country, saying her record "speaks volumes about what is in her heart." Clinton said Ginsburg's work told the public that everyone had a place in America's legal system, and that the Constitution was there to protect all people, not just the powerful.[4]

Ginsburg's goal has always been to eradicate gender-based discrimination—on any and all counts, for women but also for men. There's a famous story about a *Washington Post* reporter who interviewed Ginsburg in 1993. He saw a photograph of Ginsburg's son-in-law holding his newborn child and "gazing adoringly." The reporter says Ginsburg told her guest, "This is my dream for society . . . Fathers loving and caring for and helping raise their kids."[5]

And she did make major headway in terms of gender and the law, using a strategy like she was building a wall brick by brick, starting with *Reed v. Reed.* Susan Deller Ross, a professor at Georgetown University Law Center, once told *The New Yorker* that the court previously had a very hands-off attitude, but Ginsburg changed that, and created a judicial system that struck down laws that treated the sexes differently.[6] Ross also worked as a lawyer on sex discrimination cases in the 1970s.

Even after only a few years on the court, Ginsburg was receiving recognition for all she'd already done. In 1997, the Independent Women's Forum wrote that "the ERA has quietly and stealthily become the law of the land thanks to 25 years of Supreme Court decisions, first guided and then written by ERA advocates and now Justice Ruth Bader Ginsburg."[7]

Arthur Miller, a professor and longtime friend of the Ginsburgs (he was in the same class as Marty at Harvard Law), once said to CNN that he thinks RBG is "so far the greatest woman to be on the Supreme Court" because she "picked up the ball for women"[8] and ran with it as no one else had run before.

"She broke so many barriers, she was willing to fight, not only for women, but she was willing to fight for all the issues she cared about, access to justice, procedure equality, people," he said during an interview with CNN. "So I don't think there's much doubt that she will go down as a great justice."[9]

Due to her popularity and her staggering legacy, it is sometimes surprising that Ginsburg has been forced to field questions about when she's leaving the court for years. She became the oldest member on the bench in 2010, when the late Justice

Stevens retired at ninety after thirty-five years on the court.[10] Jeffrey Toobin said on CNN's podcast about the justice that he thinks her "failure to leave during the Obama years will be a significant part of her legacy."[11] She's faced criticism for that—people claim she should have left when Obama could have appointed another liberal judge. However, RBG slammed these criticisms as sexist—no one was demanding that the male liberal judges step down[12]—and also said that the way confirmation hearings are these days, you couldn't get somebody in who would vote the way she does.[13] However, according to the authors of *My Own Words*, Ginsburg has consistently said that for her, the test has to be, "am I equipped to do the job?" And that she will stay "as long as I can do the job full steam."[14]

There is an important lesson in her response: never let anyone or anything pressure you into quitting something you love. If you feel like you can pursue your passion to the best of your ability, keep at it, no matter what other people say.

And while there's so much to learn from RBG's legacy that will only continue to grow, the biggest and most important lesson, the one that should not be ignored, is that we should not sit back and wait for change to come. Instead, we need to pick up whatever tools we each have available to us and join RBG as she continues this fight toward a more equal and just society for all.

★ ★ ★

Of course, there is her professional legacy as a lawyer, judge, and justice.

"The one sentence is, if you want to be a successful social persuader, think of your audience and frame arguments that will appeal to the audience," Professor Joan Williams told me. "But that doesn't mean you have to lose the sharp edge of the social critique. For me, that's what is powerful about the legacy of Ruth Bader Ginsburg."

She took cases that she knew would allow the all-male panel to understand that gender discrimination hurt everyone. She framed her arguments in a way that they could not only hear, but maybe relate to.[15] The former executive director of the ACLU, Aryeh Neier, once said, "There never was another circumstance in my tenure at the ACLU when there was as clearly planned a litigation strategy as Ginsburg implemented in the women's rights field."[16] This litigation strategy ultimately contributed to many changes in American law.

Another great contribution is her encouragement for future generations to follow the path she's laid out. She once told a graduating class to use their education to provide support to their existing communities. RBG wanted the students to try do something that would provide a healthy baseline for people who came after them. "Try to leave tracks," she told them.[17]

★ ★ ★

While it is easy to assume Ginsburg's whole life is contained to her Supreme Court chambers, she does in fact have passions outside the law, and she makes time for other things and people that are important to her. Or to say it simply, as the authors of *Notorious RBG* put it, RBG gets out—a lot.[18] This is to say there is a lot more to her legacy than the way she framed arguments. Though we should all find our passion and try to make the world a better place, Ginsburg also writes handwritten thank-you notes when she has dinner at your house, she loves going to the opera, she often puts the needs of her friends above her own, and she continues to be a "loyal and generous mentor"[19] and teacher.

Judge Robert Katzmann wrote an essay that speaks to Ginsburg's essence, and he says that becoming a legend has not affected her personality. She still has a bottomless capacity for friendship and kindness, in both big and small ways, despite the burdens of her daily life. She continues to put others before herself. He gives the example of Ginsburg coming to New York City in 1999 to swear him in on the circuit court. He ends his essay by saying Ginsburg is buoyed by her work ethic and determination, and always ready to take in the simple pleasures of life.[20]

First and foremost, outside of the Supreme Court is RBG's family, something that she talks about in order to show that people can both be successful and have a family, if that's what they want. She once told *The New Yorker*'s Jeffrey Toobin that it bothered her when people point to Kagan and Sotomayor (neither of whom are married or have children) as proof that in order to succeed you have to give up a family life. But RBG has two kids, and O'Connor raised three sons.[21] Instead of comparing the four women who have sat on the court, we should acknowledge that they exemplify the idea that you can have whatever type of family and marital life you desire.

Growing up with Ruth Bader Ginsburg as a mom had its perks, of course, but she was also very demanding. RBG would redline passages from her daughter Jane's homework and "frequently ask her to rewrite them."[22] Following the release of her cousin's film *On the Basis of Sex*, Jane Ginsburg discussed her family life, her mother's high expectations for her, and how the "law was a fifth member of the family growing up" during a talk at Columbia University.

"There was never any doubt, any moment when the family thought that somehow we were being undermined or compromised because of what she was doing," Professor Ginsburg said to the *Columbia Spectator*. She said that her parents talked about everything, and when she was in high school, Jane got involved reading and even editing briefs. "It was very much a family enterprise."[23]

Jane, who now teaches at Columbia Law School in New York, still travels to Washington once a month to fill her mom's freezer with meals.[24]

RBG's idea that family matters extended into her work. This is evident from her carefree attitude if her clerks needed to pick up their kids (and especially loved when fathers were taking on that role). She also altered the way the ACLU dealt with children. In her book *Ruth Bader Ginsburg: A Life,* author Jane De Hart talks about how at the time Ginsburg founded the ACLU's Women's Rights Project in 1972, it was not typical for people to bring their children to the workplace. Ginsburg changed that, and made sure kids felt welcome in the WRP's offices. One time, one of the male founders of the ACLU walked into the Women's Rights Project to ask a young lawyer a question and was surprised to find her sitting there breastfeeding a baby.[25]

★ ★ ★

When RBG found out that clerk Paul Schiff Berman was dating someone who clerked for another justice in the Supreme Court, she buzzed him into her chambers. Ginsburg then said,

"I didn't know you had a special friend at the court! You must have her up for tea." So Berman told his then-girlfriend Laura, who was clerking for Justice Breyer and Justice Blackmun, that she needed to come meet his boss in an almost "meet-the-parents" type way. The couple spent thirty minutes with the justice (who did have tea prepared). Years later, Ginsburg performed the couple's wedding ceremony, Berman told me on the phone (he has shared this story multiple times with journalists and authors) and where the officiant says "by the power vested in me," Ginsburg said, "By the power vested in me by the US Constitution, I now pronounce you husband and wife."

"[That] always makes Laura and me laugh because it means if we got divorced it might be unconstitutional," Berman recounted. Ginsburg is known for using this phrase at weddings—she said the same when she officiated her nephew's wedding,[26] and again at the wedding of Michal Kahn and Charles Mitchem.[27]

These stories exemplify the idea that in an ideal world, you should fill your life with people who support and encourage you. RBG built strong friendships and good working relationships with the people in her chambers. There is of course a sliding scale of how close Ginsburg gets to her clerks, but there is no doubt that she cares deeply for them all. And Berman is not the only person who married someone they met at the court. Former clerk Margo Schlanger, one of Ginsburg's first clerks at the Supreme Court, credits Ginsburg with both helping her figure out how to create a career that allowed her to be both a civil rights lawyer and a law professor, and also with finding her husband.

"I am not sure if I would've married my husband if it hadn't been for RBG; she's really been a very dominant presence for me," Schlanger said to me. She and her husband, Samuel Bagenstos, met professionally while Schlanger was working at a job Ginsburg had helped her get. Bagenstos was heading to clerk for Ginsburg, and Schlanger had recently finished her clerkship.

"She likes her step-clerks to get along, so we got to be friends as a result of that connection and then we eventually got married," Schlanger said. "In terms of where [Ginsburg] is in my life, I am pretty clear: she's super important, my life would've been completely different."

Nearly every clerk I spoke to said that Ginsburg impacted and helped their careers, and many of them said they have stayed in touch long past the end of the clerkship. But even more than that, they told me that Ginsburg makes sure to send a note when her clerks get a new job or get married—and she is also sure to send along an "RBG grandclerk" T-shirt that includes the Supreme Court seal when they have a new baby.[28] The notoriously stern justice once even participated in clerk fantasy baseball, the *Notorious RBG* authors revealed.[29]

★ ★ ★

Have I mentioned yet that Ginsburg loves the opera? Of the approximately twenty interviews I did for this book, nearly every single person mentioned that RBG is a big fan of it (though I did already know this—when I reported on her talk with Totenberg in December 2018, Ginsburg said the thing she missed most about New York was the Metropolitan Opera, which has "no rival in the world"). When the Ginsburgs lived in Oklahoma, they would drive four hours to Dallas in order to hear the Metropolitan Opera's traveling performance.[30] Now,

RBG oversees twice-annual opera and instrumental recitals at the court, as they give her a break from the heaviness of her court duties.[31] It is just one example of how Ginsburg makes time for other enjoyable things in her life.

"With her, it was particularly classical music, especially opera but really classical music more generally, and she took time to go to festivals that she wanted to see, even though she was working these crazy hours, she didn't let the crazy hours mean that she had nothing else going on, she always made time for other things," Schlanger told me. "Not a ton of time, I don't want to exaggerate, but always a little time."

Then there's her workout routine. Ginsburg got a trainer after her colon-cancer surgery. In December 2018, Ginsburg was recovering from a fall the month before in which she broke three ribs. Even so, when Totenberg asked about her health, RBG made sure to tell the crowd that she was already back to doing her whole workout routine, which includes push-ups and weighted curls. When she works out, she usually listens to "opera recordings," (what a shock) and when Stephen Colbert tried to play different music when he joined her for a workout one day, she told him she would "never ever exercise to that noise."[32]

Though her quiet demeanor and her love of opera might paint one type of picture, she is actually quite the daredevil. In her earlier years, she loved waterskiing and horseback riding; she has been known to go paddleboarding, and then there is the time that she and Justice Scalia were in the French Riviera for a summer teaching gig and she went parasailing.

"Ruth—honest to goodness—went up behind a motor boat," Scalia said of the trip. "I mean, she's so light you would think she would never come down. I would not do that."[33]

She also maintains a sense of humor, which might be a little startling to many who have only witnessed the stern-faced, quiet woman on the bench. It also might come as a surprise to her children, who when they were young kept a notebook called "Mommy Laughed." Her daughter, Jane, dryly remarks in the *RBG* documentary that "it had parsimonious entries."[34] But RBG does find Kate McKinnon's impersonation on *SNL* "marvelously funny,"[35] for one thing (though the only part of the impersonation that Ginsburg said reminds her of herself is the collar) and she is known to crack jokes; you just have to pay attention.

"She actually has quite a good sense of humor, you have to listen closely to catch it, but she has a very sly, flinty sense of humor sometimes which was really funny when it came out," former clerk Paul Schiff Berman said.

Totenberg once wrote that classic RBG meant "tough and to the point, with a touch of gallows humor."[36]

★ ★ ★

Based on everything we know, trying to be more like Ruth Bader Ginsburg can feel like an impossible task, because she just seems so untouchable, especially now thanks to the fame that she has accumulated over the years. In fact, what makes RBG notorious has been there all along, and Ginsburg is probably more surprised by anyone that people want to take pictures with a woman in her eighties.

"She's no different now than she was twenty-five years ago or twenty years ago," said Nina Totenberg to me, "it's just that people somehow, maybe it was the Notorious RBG, maybe it was the T-shirts, but I don't quite know, but it multiplies exponentially, so the more stuff about her, the more people know about her, and there's very little that's not admirable about Ruth Bader Ginsburg. The truth is, she's a wonderful human being."

To the people who know her best, watching her become a rock star was an experience in itself. Schlanger said that watching Justice Ginsburg become the Notorious RBG was a "hoot."

"Here was somebody who had been so important in my life and who I admired as one of the very best lawyers in the country and a fantastic justice, but all of a sudden she became an icon," said Schlanger. "People call people icons all the time, that's a word that gets overused a lot, but all of a sudden it actually became true, and it was a hoot to watch."

Schlanger told me that she once tried to buy a Ruth Bader Ginsburg bobblehead for her office at the University of Michigan, where she teaches law. However, because everyone wanted to buy one, they were incredibly expensive. That was when Schlanger realized how big of a pop-culture icon Ginsburg had become.

"I knew why I wanted her bobblehead in my office, but there weren't many people like me who had that reason, and so all of a sudden it was like, oh you know what, this is a real thing," she said.

It's not exactly clear where this social icon status came from. Maybe it was in her dissents, the creation of the Notorious RBG blog, or the big frocks she wears on the court? Or were people just looking for a hero in dark times? That's definitely part of it.

"We're also just in the age where women are looking for heroes, and she's an obvious candidate, especially when she reads these ringing dissents from the bench, because the younger women feel a sense of entitlement to be assertive and to demand their rights," said Joan Williams, a professor at UC Hastings College of the Law.

Maybe part of it is just being at the right place at the right time, former clerk David Post pondered during our interview.

"She's become a symbol because people need a symbol of something she represents and I think she embraces that, not in a crazy way or an egotistical way, but that's who she is now, and I think she's comfortable with that . . . because that is the role [she's] playing in this society now," he said. "I think it takes an odd kind of courage to do that."

Though the justice may be the most surprised by her sudden rise to fame, most people I spoke to felt like she enjoys it, yes, but also that she thinks it is important for a multitude of reasons.

"I think she's very surprised that she has become an icon," said journalist Marvin Kalb. "That was not her intent. She became an icon probably one because of her, well, iconic contribution to our society at this particular point. And the second point is timing. She doesn't create the timing, she didn't create Trump, she didn't create disfunction in the US government. But she feels that she can make a contribution of a positive nature toward improving our society by pushing the outer boundaries of the law to achieve gender equality and full gender opportunity."

Her notorious status has made Ginsburg, the second ever female judge on the highest court in the land, more visible, which in turn gives women and young girls the ability to see themselves in whatever role they may want—an opportunity she did not have when she was young and an opportunity that was denied to her mother.

"I think part of the reason she likes having become the notorious RBG and all the attention she's gained in recent years is that it's a way for her to connect with a younger generation of women," Berman continued.

Ginsburg frequently talks about the idea that people learn from seeing and experience. For example, she has said that the reason Chief Justice Rehnquist was sympathetic toward the Family and Medical Leave Act was that he had to take care of his grandchildren when his daughter was working, and he saw a need for support in child rearing.[37]

During a 2008 speech, Ginsburg said that judges do read the newspaper and are swayed "by the climate of the era."[38]

These ideas, that visibility affects others and that the Supreme Court responds to social change, make up important parts of her legacy and point toward the biggest lesson that we can learn from her—in order to create legal change, you have to create social change.

In the 1970s, Supreme Court justices and judges around the nation were alerted to a change in America's society, Ginsburg wrote in the foreword of the 2001 Women's Rights Project annual report. There was a shift in the work women wanted to do, and the family care men wanted to share.

"The Justices' still imperfect but ever evolving enlightenment has been advanced by the briefs filed in Court, the women lawyers and jurists they nowadays routinely encounter, and perhaps most deeply by the aspirations of the women, particularly the daughters and granddaughters, in their own families and communities," she writes.[39]

And RBG does not want the court to get ahead of public opinion. When people were upset in the 1980s that the court was not willing to elevate gender to the level of a suspect class after a decade of challenges, Ginsburg had a message for those who "hoped for too much too soon." She remained optimistic that a "continued focus on the social and economic trends in society . . . would exert pressure on lawmakers."[40]

The justice has called the court a "reactive institution" and has said that the court is pushed by society, not the other way around.

"It's never in the forefront for social change, there's always a movement in society that's pushing the court that way. When you think of *Brown v. Board* and the campaign, it was not only that Thurgood Marshall was the building lawyer and made building blocks to get up to *Brown v. Board,* it was the tenor of the times," Ginsburg said during an interview with professor Joan Williams at UC Berkeley. She explains that the United States had just fought against racism in the Second World War, but most troops during the war were separated by race. After the war, it was apparent that the racism American troops were fighting against abroad existed back home. Things needed to change.[41]

The timing needs to be right, and unfortunately, that means we have to get comfortable with things not changing at the drop of a hat. Similarly, when Ginsburg started fighting for women's rights in the 1970s, the movement was happening both in the United States and around the world, and people cared about the issue.

"Judges had daughters and granddaughters and they began to recognize that some of, some of the so-called favors for women were not favors at all but they were locking women into a small piece of men's wide world," Ginsburg once said about why the time was right in the 1970s for her to fight for equality. This change in society helped open the court's eyes and made the arguments Ginsburg was making acceptable, when they had not been the generation prior.[42]

She has frequently said that although she agreed with the outcome and result of the court's decision in *Roe v. Wade*, she thinks the opinion went "too far too fast" and should have just invalidated the one extreme Texas law at that time and made steadier change. The decision "cut off the political process, which had been slowly liberalizing the laws state by state."[43] Some feminists have not been thrilled with this critique.[44]

★ ★ ★

All of this is to say that in order for us to help Ginsburg continue her legacy, and in order for us to make our own, we all need to help create social change—we have to create that "feedback loop."[45] When Ginsburg started the ACLU Women's Rights Project, her team had three missions: public education, to make people care about the change; the legislature, and getting it to change; and finally, the courts. Ginsburg said they worked on all three levels to create change.[46]

"In Alexander Hamilton's words, the mission of judges is 'to secure a steady, upright, and impartial administration of the laws,'" Ginsburg said during her Senate confirmation hearing opening statement. "I would add that the judge should carry out that function without fanfare, but with due care. She should decide the case before her without reaching out to cover cases not yet seen."[47]

There are many people who are hoping Ginsburg can "save" us, going so far as offering ribs when she fell and broke hers or internal organs when it was announced she had cancer surgery.[48] But what "the public perceives as reasonable and fair plays a role in judicial decisions."[49] And while her staying healthy and on the Supreme Court is very important to many people (me included!), one lesson that we should all remember is that she didn't do this alone. She spent the 1970s fighting alongside her ACLU colleagues and expanding on work that others had done.

And though we watched her create so much change over her lifetime, former clerk Berman thinks it is important to note that the Supreme Court operates best when it is responding to social change in society and articulating principles to solidify that change, not leading change itself. Therefore, the lesson we can take away from the legacy of RBG is none other than the idea that we should follow in her footsteps and fight for what we believe in if we want to see legal and large changes in society.

Ginsburg has said that she has found it most satisfying to be a part of a movement that made life better for everyone. The Constitution starts off by talking about the people of the United States forming a more perfect union. RBG believes we are still striving for that perfect union, and in order to get there, "we the people" needs to be a consistently growing group.[50]

One time, Berman brought his then-thirteen-year-old son to meet his former boss after oral argument. Berman told Justice Ginsburg that his son was very "disillusioned" with the political situation in the United States at the time, and he asked Ginsburg if she had any advice for his son about how best to understand that moment in history.

"And she said that her husband always used to say that the symbol of America is not the bald eagle, it's the pendulum, and that pendulum swings in both directions over time. That really captures Justice Ginsburg's perspective; she always takes the long view," Berman told me.

Dahlia Lithwick said that when Ginsburg talks about those whose shoulders she has stood on, she is saying "this kind of story that we tell of her greatness is not the story, and that the story is she achieved what she achieved because amazing men and women gave her opportunities, and that we are way too in love with the idea in this country of the 'great savior' who reaches and changes everything."

What Ginsburg wants people to do more than she wants them to buy the tote bags and the T-shirts, Lithwick continued, is "to be part of a collective that does something, in my view, that can mean going to law school, it can mean running for office, it can be writing op-eds for the paper, but it's just the opposite of passive hero worship. I think that she would be the first person to say that passive hero worship gets you kind of nowhere, but massive collective organizing and institutional work changes the world."

"I think she would probably also say that even in moments like this one, where it's hard to be a woman and to see the arc of the moral universe going in the wrong direction," Lithwick continued, "it's not the time to sort of sit back and wring your hands but it's time to double down on work she started in the 1960s and 1970s, and I think that she's just not a person who gives up and not a person who sort of waits for someone else to save you either."

★ ★ ★

This isn't easy, of course, especially when the fight feels futile. Creating change is slow, boring, and painstaking work.

But you have to do the actual work. While traveling to the University of California at Berkeley in 2013, Ginsburg saw law students in "Notorious R.B.G." shirts. She asked them to "fight for the things they care about, do it in a way that will lead others to join them, and maintain a sense of humor." She knows that progress is seldom linear.[51]

Ginsburg continues to use her celebrity to speak on issues that are important to her. She once presided over a naturalization ceremony for thirty-one people at the New-York Historical Society. She told the audience the country is "made strong by people like you" and shared the story of her dad immigrating at age thirteen from Russia with no money and no English skills. She went on to "urge the newest citizens to vote, foster unity, and make America better."[52]

So, if you want to be like the Notorious RBG, you must follow this path that she laid out: roll up your sleeves, do the work (and do it well) to create change through incremental steps. Don't give up when things get hard, but instead adjust your plan to overcome obstacles. Help jump-start social movements so that the law will follow. It is important to share her words and her work in order to bring attention to what she is doing. But it is more important to begin or continue doing the work yourself. Work within your community to create lasting and real change and build your own legacy.

I asked former clerk Goodwin Liu, now an associate justice of the Supreme Court of California, what he thought Justice Ginsburg would say to those waiting for her to save them.

"She would say don't wait for me to save anybody, she would say you gotta roll your sleeves up and get to work. I'm sure that's what she would say," he said on the phone. "She does not cast herself as a savior of anyone. She understands her role as someone who inspires and motivates but she's also conscious that there's a lot of hard work that has to be done by a lot of people for anything to change in this world. She has been in the trenches herself and done that work, and so she's not under any illusion that one person can wave a magic wand, even a wand as powerful as hers."

Therefore, let's get to work. I think the only fitting way to end this book is to leave you with the honorable Justice Ruth Bader Ginsburg's own words, said to Irin Carmon in 2015, on who she would like to be remembered as:

> *"Someone who used whatever talent she had to do her work to the very best of her ability. And to help repair the tears in her society, to make things a little better through the use of whatever ability she has."*[53]

A Quick Guide to Lessons Learned

1. Find your passion and pursue it.
   a. But it's okay to have more than one!
2. Hard work pays off. Find when and where you work best and get to it.
3. Turn in your best work, every time.
4. Have a plan, but be prepared to adjust it when obstacles or challenges arise.
5. Looking at what other people/countries/organizations have done can help you figure out that plan, and can provide guidelines for what has worked and what hasn't.
6. If you decide to have a lifelong partner (however you define partner), find one like Marty—someone who thinks your career is just as important as theirs, someone who makes you laugh, someone who doesn't see building a life together as a sacrifice.

7. Friendships are important—and you can maintain them despite political differences.
   a. Ways to maintain friendships:
      i. Eat good food together, embrace your similarities and shared interests, say thank you, support each other through the ups and downs that life presents, focus on what matters.
8. Always recognize those on whose shoulders you stand.
   a. Do this for people who paved the way and people who are currently on the path with you.
9. In times of hardship, going back to work or getting back on a schedule can help you stay afloat.
   a. Continue the battle, if you can.
   b. But if this doesn't work for you, don't do it. Put your health and well-being first and find what is best for you.
10. It's okay to be angry, but find a way to utilize that anger to persuade others to create positive change.
    a. People might be more willing to listen if you're not yelling.
    b. Being angry will affect your ability to convince people that they should be on your team.
11. And when persuasion doesn't work: Dissent.
    a. Dissent loudly, dissent clearly, dissent with the goal of creating a response.
12. We cannot just wait for our idols to save us. We need to roll up our sleeves and do the work to make active change in society, so that the court and the law can follow.

Acknowledgments

THIS BOOK WOULD NOT HAVE been possible without the endless support, encouragement, and help of my friends and family. Writing a book was all at once exhausting, exhilarating, impactful, and educational. I wrote it from coffee shops and friends' houses around the country, on planes, the floors of airports, hotels, and in multiple co-working spaces. I woke up in the middle of the night with ideas, and I deleted almost every sentence I wrote at least once. And throughout this process there have been lonely days, overwhelming days, boring days, exciting days. There were days I was convinced I wouldn't actually publish a single word. But then there were days where I had amazing interviews with people I highly admire and respect. And through it all, I had my community. I am endlessly grateful for the people in my life, people who consistently show up for me at the most stressful times, thrilling times, hard times, happy times. I don't think I can adequately thank everyone who helped with this book (I also don't think that when my editor said I owed her 50,000 words she realized my acknowledgments section could be that alone), but I will try. Of course, recognizing those who helped you get to where you are is part of the RBG way.

First of all, the biggest and most important thank-you must go to Justice Ruth Bader Ginsburg herself, who has spent her life fighting for equality and justice, and it is in part because of her that I am able to be the writer and feminist that I am today. Thank you for inspiring us, for dedicating your life to others, for giving us these lessons. I am grateful for your dissents, for your gallows humor, for your dedication and strength. I learned so much from you, and I hope to be able to emulate even just a few of your traits and skills throughout my life.

A huge thank-you to everyone who agreed to speak to me for this book. I sent over sixty-five interview requests over the course of writing, and I am so grateful to those clerks, authors, journalists, and experts who found time to share their knowledge and insight, off the record or on. I cannot thank you all enough for your help and for the information and stories that you shared. Each interview was invaluable.

To my editor, Julie Ganz, and to Skyhorse Publishing: Thank you for asking me to write this book and for giving me this opportunity. Julie, I will never forget the first email you sent (I am so glad it wasn't spam). Since then, you have changed the trajectory of my career, and I am so happy to have been able to work with you. Thank you for always answering my many, many questions, and for being so helpful throughout this process.

I am the writer and reporter I am because of the mentors I have been lucky enough to have throughout my career thus far. Willa Seidenberg and Alan Mittelstaedt, thank you for always being there when I need you, for pushing me to dream bigger. Marvin Kalb, I am grateful for your guidance (and for your interview!). To Mylène Dressler: Thank you for your support and advice when this book was first becoming a reality. Your excitement made it all feel real.

And to Jeff Jeske, my forever hero, guardian, friend, adviser. There will never be enough ways to thank you for all you did—I would not be writing a book today without you, and I thought about you a lot during this process. I really wish I could have shared it with you. We all miss you.

And to my friends. You made me laugh when I was feeling down, you made me work hard even when I wanted to be hanging out with you all, you encouraged me and lifted me up. To the many people who checked in, who texted me words of encouragement, whose excitement and support and bragging to others about me made me feel like I really could do this, thank you. I want to extend a thank-you to my community overall, because even if you did not directly impact this book, you impacted my life by being in it and being my friend, so thank you for that.

To Rachael Cerrotti, Meghan Dhaliwal, and Dominic Bracco: The three of you and the work you each do give me constant hope and inspiration. To my HEFAT team, our group message is oftentimes the best part of my week and I aspire to be like each one of you.

Cody Tracey, I am always grateful for your boundless energy and light in my life. Thank you for being you.

Josephine LaBua, you are the person who taught me just how notorious the Notorious RBG really is, and I am forever grateful. I'm so proud of the way you live your life. I love you, and you're important to me. Melissa Woods and Lauren Hoy, I appreciate your love and friendship more than you realize.

Marisa Simkin and Justin Rhoades, you provided a home for me to work in, beer for me to celebrate with, and support that kept me buoyed. Laura Schultze, thank you for your constant kindness and encouragement. Sean Myers, thank you for a friendship that has spanned multiple cities and timezones.

Ani Ucar, you astound me on the daily with your skills, talent and drive. I can't wait to report with you again someday.

Holly Thompson, you magical being. I admire your work ethic, your optimism, your ability to see the good in things. I am in awe of you and lucky to know you.

Sara Tiano: I don't know what I would do without you in my life. I am so grateful for every single gift you have given me over the years: Friendship, laughter, a stern talking to when I need it, a warm home, a supportive ear, and so much more.

Diana Crandall, you and I have truly worked more jobs and projects together in more places than I ever could have imagined. Thank you for always being there (and for your keen eye, multiple rereadings, your suggestions, and your fact-checks!). I am so grateful for your friendship and support that has remained consistent no matter where we are in the world.

Martha Daniel, my main BBQ. Thank you for your support and hugs and giggles and encouragement. I am so lucky to be able to turn to you on both coasts. Jake Salley, thank you for the laughter and the cocktails and the best nickname.

A big lesson I personally learned during this process: Get yourself a friend with whom you can make an accountability spreadsheet, because it is a game-changer. Daniel Raeder, your friendship and love means more to me than you can ever know, and the fact that I could turn to you and ask for help means the world. Thank you for being you.

To my roommate: Amanda Ottaway, thank you for being there for me through the death-defying bus rides, the laughter and the tears, the hikes to get to the hikes, the small and big joys, and all the Carroll Gardens patios (ours especially). There's no one I would rather share this monster city with.

To Becca King, you had the number one best reaction to me writing this book. You have always given me such sincere validation and advice, since day one of freshmen year. We've figured out so many important life lessons together and for that, I am so grateful.

Erin Reitz, I don't know where I would be without our friendship. Thank you for being in my life, for consistently and gently showing me the way. I have the upmost respect and admiration for you.

And to Becca and Erin both: Thank you for giving me the break I needed toward the end of this journey and thank you for literally and figuratively lifting each other and me up in our times of need.

Becky Girardot and Adelle Grant-McCauley Trout. You are the two best friends a girl could ask for and I look up to you both in more ways than I can count. Becky, you radiate joy, and your friendship and love gives me energy. Adelle, your friendship is my rock. I am beyond-words grateful that we have been by each other's sides for coming up on two decades.

Okay, deep breath. Moving on to my family. To all the Gibians and the Crumms: You are all my pillars and guiding stars throughout everything I do. I love you all and am so grateful for your endless support and encouragement.

To Grandma Dot and Pop-pop, who taught me how to be brave, to love breakfast food, to believe in myself, to be kind and generous, and to always keep a sense of humor. To Grandma Peg and Granddad, who instilled in me a love of travel, a desire to always keep learning, and the lessons of simplicity, love, and friendship.

I think I can honestly say I am the luckiest little sibling in the world. I am so proud to call myself their sister. Thank you for being my friends and my siblings. I love you.

To my sisters, Carrie and Rachel: Thank you for paving the way for me. Thank you for teaching me what it means to be strong. Thank you for letting me lean on you when I need it. Thank you for letting me ramble on and on about feminism and journalism. Thank you for being the best role models I could ever have. To my brother, Davey: You have never questioned my dreams or decisions and have instead consistently made moves to help me realize them. You don't just support and encourage me, but you actively take steps to help me get one step further. Thank you for never wavering in your support. I am so proud of all you do (the parts I understand).

And to their spouses: Miles, Mark, and Maria. I love that you are all part of the family. Thank you for the car rides, the vacations, the pictures in the family group text. You are all so kind, so supportive, so smart, and so encouraging. Thank you for making my siblings so happy.

And finally, to my parents. Mom and Dad, thank you for everything you always do for me. You read chapters, you listened quietly while I stress-vented, you encouraged me when things felt hard. Throughout my whole life, you have never told me that I couldn't do something. You have only ever provided the space for me to go one step further. Thank you both for your honesty, your love, your humor, and your support, for the countless lessons you taught me and continue teaching me. Dad, you taught me to never be afraid to try new things and you inspired me to always be a trouper. Mom, you showed me what a strong, independent woman is. Your work ethic; your dedication to your students, family, and friends; your commitment to education; your love for us—these things do not go unnoticed. I love you both lots and lots and lots and lots.

I am who I am because of the shoulders I stand on. A final thank-you to the people who have fought for equality for decades. Thank you to the women who have broken down barriers and paved the way for us all to follow.

APPENDIX A
List of Sources

BELOW IS A LIST OF people whom I interviewed on the record*
for this book. I want to thank each of them for their time,
stories, and help. Their interviews were invaluable, and I can
honestly say I couldn't have done this book without them.
Organized in alphabetical order by first name.

1. Barbara Babcock, pioneer of the study of women and the
   law
2. Dahlia Lithwick, senior editor and legal correspondent for *Slate*
3. David Post, former clerk
4. Frank Askin, RBG's former student at Rutgers and her
   former colleague at the ACLU and Rutgers former student
   at Rutgers
5. Justice Goodwin Liu, former clerk
6. Heather Elliott, former clerk
7. Jane De Hart, author of *Ruth Bader Ginsburg: A Life*

8. Jay Wexler, former clerk
9. Joan Williams, lawyer and professor, expert in women and the law
10. Lenora Lapidus, former executive director of the ACLU Women's Project (sadly, Lapidus passed away from breast cancer a couple of months after we spoke)
11. Margo Schlanger, former clerk
12. Marvin Kalb, journalist, author, and RBG acquaintance
13. Nina Totenberg, NPR's legal correspondent and RBG friend
14. Paul Berman, former clerk
15. Ruthanne Deutsch, former clerk
16. Stephanie Wildman, editor of *Women in the Law*
17. Scott Dodson, editor of *The Legacy of Ruth Bader Ginsburg*

*Note: I did speak to people off the record or on background for this book for numerous reasons.

Notes

Note: All page numbers apply to the print versions of the books they reference.

Introduction

1. "... where she was one of only nine women, seated among about 500 men."—Ginsburg, Ruth Bader; Hartnett, Mary; Williams, Wendy W. *My Own Words*. Timeline at beginning of book (Pg. 1). New York: Simon & Schuster, 2016.

2. "... the Harvard Law Review and Columbia Law Review."—"Celebrating Women's History Month: America's First Women in Law." *Aon Attorneys Advantage*. Created March 2019. https://www.attorneys-advantage.com/Risk-Management/Americas-First-Women-in-Law (Accessed 21 June 2019).

3. "... which fulfilled their commitment to diversity."—De Hart, Jane Sherron. *Ruth Bader Ginsburg*. Pg. 78. New York: Alfred A. Knopf, Penguin Random House, 2018.

4. "... two second interviews and no job offers."—De Hart, Jane Sherron. *Ruth Bader Ginsburg*. Pg. 78. New York: Alfred A. Knopf, Penguin Random House, 2018.

5. "... they shared an interest in process theory."—De Hart, Jane Sherron. *Ruth Bader Ginsburg*. Pg. 80. New York: Alfred A. Knopf, Penguin Random House, 2018.

6. ". . . wouldn't even interview."—Totenberg, Nina. "Notes on a Life" in *The Legacy of Ruth Bader Ginsburg,* ed. Scott Dodson. Pg. 5. (New York: Cambridge University Press, 2015), 3–12.

7. ". . . Thurgood Marshall of the women's movement."—Born, Brooksley. "The 2016 Justice Ruth Bader Ginsburg Distinguished Lecture on Women and the Law by Brooksley Born." New York City Bar. 15 min, 34 sec. into video. Created 18 February 2016. https://www.nycbar.org/media-listing/media/detail/the-2016-justice-ruth-bader-ginsburg-distinguished-lecture-on-women-and-the-law-by-brooksley-born (Accessed 20 June 2019).

8. ". . . history of the Republic."—Hirsham, Linda. *Sisters in Law.* Pg. 44. New York: HarperCollins, 2015.

9. ". . . no separate categories for genders."—Hirsham, Linda. *Sisters in Law.* Pg. 57. New York: HarperCollins, 2015.

10. ". . . just out of reach."—De Hart, Jane Sherron. *Ruth Bader Ginsburg.* Pg. xiii. New York: Alfred A. Knopf, Penguin Random House, 2018.

Part I: Fighting for Equality

1. ". . . object of discrimination."—Sherr, Lynn. *The Record,* Vol. 56, No. 1. Pg. 21. Created Winter 2001. https://www2.nycbar.org/Publications/record/winter01.1.pdf (Accessed 9 May 2019).

Chapter 1: On When There Are Nine

1. ". . . 1 First Street NE in Washington, DC"—De Hart, Jane Sherron. *Ruth Bader Ginsburg.* Pg. 204–5. New York: Alfred A. Knopf, Penguin Random House, 2018.

2. ". . . both unfair and senseless."—De Hart, Jane Sherron. *Ruth Bader Ginsburg.* Pg. 113. New York: Alfred A. Knopf, Penguin Random House, 2018.

3. ". . . male service members."—De Hart, Jane Sherron. *Ruth Bader Ginsburg.* Pg. 199. New York: Alfred A. Knopf, Penguin Random House, 2018.

4. ". . . barely 100-pound lawyer."—De Hart, Jane Sherron. *Ruth Bader Ginsburg.* Pg. 349. New York: Alfred A. Knopf, Penguin Random House, 2018.

5. ". . . take their feet off our necks."—Ruiz, Michelle. "15 Things I Learned About Ruth Bader Ginsburg From *Notorious RBG.*"

Vogue. Created 29 October 2015. https://www.vogue.com/article /ruth-bader-ginsburg-notorious-rbg-book (Accessed 20 June 2019).

6. ". . . profoundly silent."—De Hart, Jane Sherron. *Ruth Bader Ginsburg.* Pg. 207. New York: Alfred A. Knopf, Penguin Random House, 2018.

7. ". . . sex discrimination in history."—De Hart, Jane Sherron. *Ruth Bader Ginsburg.* Pg. 216. New York: Alfred A. Knopf, Penguin Random House, 2018.

8. ". . . for American women."—West, Besty and Cohen, Julie. *RBG.* 3:40 to 3:48. https://www.cnn.com/shows/rbg-ruth-bader-ginsburg -film (Accessed 19 June 2019).

9. ". . . go to law school," and ". . . hired her as his assistant."—Ginsburg, Ruth Bader; Hartnett, Mary; Williams, Wendy W. Pg. 20–21. *My Own Words.* Pg. 21. New York: Simon & Schuster, 2016.

10. ". . . consciousness raiser."—Ginsburg, Ruth Bader; Hartnett, Mary; Williams, Wendy W. Pg. 21. *My Own Words.* Pg. 21. New York: Simon & Schuster, 2016.

11. ". . . even make things better."—Ginsburg, Ruth Bader; Hartnett, Mary; Williams, Wendy W. Pg. 21. *My Own Words.* New York: Simon & Schuster, 2016.

12. ". . . community and the nation."—"At the US Supreme Court: A Conversation with Justice Ruth Bader Ginsburg." *Stanford Lawyer* 89. Created 11 November 2013. https://law.stanford.edu/stanford-lawyer/ articles/legal-matters/ (Accessed 21 June 2019).

13. ". . . marginalized people."—Hirsham, Linda. *Sisters in Law.* Pg. 11. New York: HarperCollins, 2015.

14. ". . . do her coursework."—Carmon, Irin, and Knizhnik, Shana. *Notorious RBG: The Life and Times of Ruth Bader Ginsburg.* Pg. 28. New York: HarperCollins, 2015.

15. ". . . federal appellate court."—Ginsburg, Ruth Bader; Hartnett, Mary; Williams, Wendy W. *My Own Words.* Pg. xvi. New York: Simon & Schuster, 2016.

16. ". . . from a qualified man."—Galanes, Philip. "Ruth Bader Ginsburg and Gloria Steinem on the Unending Fight for Women's Rights," Table for Three, *New York Times.* Created 14 November 2015. https://www. nytimes.com/2015/11/15/fashion/ruth-bader-ginsburg-and-gloria- steinem-on-the-unending-fight-for-womens-rights.html (Accessed 20 June 2019).

17. ". . . academic semester."—Ginsburg, Ruth Bader; Hartnett, Mary; Williams, Wendy W. *My Own Words.* Pg. 72. New York: Simon & Schuster, 2016.

18. ". . . Association of American Law Schools."—Ginsburg, Ruth Bader; Hartnett, Mary; Williams, Wendy W. *My Own Words.* Pg. 72. New York: Simon & Schuster, 2016.

19. ". . . concept of martial rape."—De Hart, Jane Sherron. *Ruth Bader Ginsburg.* Pg. 109. New York: Alfred A. Knopf, Penguin Random House, 2018.

20. ". . . prior to 1970."—Schneider, Elizabeth and Wildman, Stephanie. *Women and the Law.* Pg. 5. New York: Thomson Reuters Foundation Press, 2011.

21. ". . . fifty states until 1975."—Weaver, Warren Jr., "High Court Backs Women's Jury Rights," *New York Times.* Created 22 January 1975. https://www.nytimes.com/1975/01/22/archives/high-court-backs-womens-jury-rights-supreme-court-supports-the.html (Accessed 10 May 2019)

22. ". . . into a US military academy."—Schloesser, Kelly. "The first women of West Point." Website of the US Army, 27 October 2010. https://www.army.mil/article/47238/the_first_women_of_west_point (Accessed 10 May 2019).

23. ". . . cosign their application."—Eveleth, Rose. "Forty Years Ago, Women Had a Hard Time Getting Credit Cards." *Smithsonian Magazine.* Created 8 January 2014. https://www.smithsonianmag.com/smart-news/forty-years-ago-women-had-a-hard-time-getting-credit-cards-180949289/?no-ist (Accessed 10 May 2019).

24. ". . . rent an apartment."—Galanes, Philip. "Ruth Bader Ginsburg and Gloria Steinem on the Unending Fight for Women's Rights," Table for Three, *New York Times.* Created 14 November 2015. https://www.nytimes.com/2015/11/15/fashion/ruth-bader-ginsburg-and-gloria-steinem-on-the-unending-fight-for-womens-rights.html (Accessed 10 May 2019).

25. ". . . would not get tenure."—Totenberg, Nina. "Notes on a Life" in *The Legacy of Ruth Bader Ginsburg,* ed. Scott Dodson. Pg. 5. (New York: Cambridge University Press, 2015), 3–12.

26. ". . . who got pregnant." Pregnancy Discrimination Act of 1978, USC, 31 October 1978. On the website of the US Equal Employment

Opportunity Commission. https://www.eeoc.gov/laws/statutes/pregnancy.cfm (Accessed 10 May 2019).

27. ". . . Pregnancy Discrimination Act."—Schama, Chloe, "Ruth Bader Ginsburg Hero for Pregnant Women," *Elle*, 5 November 2015. https://www.elle.com/culture/career-politics/news/a31721/ruth-bader-ginsburg-hero-for-pregnant-women/ (Accessed 10 May 2019).

28. ". . . jury service for women."—"Edwards v. Healy." *Oyez*, www.oyez.org/cases/1974/73–759. Accessed 19 Jun. 2019.

29. ". . . in the country."—Olson, Elizabeth. , "Women Make Up Majority of U.S. Law Students for the First Time," *New York Times*. Created 16 December 2016. https://www.nytimes.com/2016/12/16/business/dealbook/women-majority-of-us-law-students-first-time.html (Accessed 9 May 2019).

30. ". . . are now women." Day, Jennifer Cheeseman, "More than 1 in 3 Lawyers are Women," United States Census Bureau. Created 8 May 2018. https://www.census.gov/library/stories/2018/05/women-lawyers.html. (Accessed 9 May 2019).

31. ". . . cut from the same mold."—Williams, Brenna. "#TBT: Ruth Bader Ginsburg becomes a Supreme Court justice." CNN. Created 21 August 2018. https://edition.cnn.com/2018/08/09/politics/ruth-bader-ginsburg-swearing-in-tbt/index.html (Accessed 31 May 2019).

32. ". . . from 1961–1963."—Ginsburg, Ruth Bader; Hartnett, Mary; Williams, Wendy W. *My Own Words*. Time line at beginning of book (Pg. 1). New York: Simon & Schuster, 2016.

33. ". . . exposed to Swedish law."—Galanes, Philip. "Ruth Bader Ginsburg and Gloria Steinem on the Unending Fight for Women's Rights." *New York Times*. Created 14 November 2015. https://www.nytimes.com/2015/11/15/fashion/ruth-bader-ginsburg-and-gloria-steinem-on-the-unending-fight-for-womens-rights.html (Accessed 10 May 2019).

34. ". . . Rutgers School of Law." Ginsburg, Ruth Bader; Hartnett, Mary; Williams, Wendy W. *My Own Words*. Time line at beginning of book (Pg. 1). New York: Simon & Schuster, 2016.

35. ". . . we felt empowered."—Rafei, Roya. "Ruth Bader Ginsburg: The Former Rutgers Law Professor Led the Legal Campaign for Gender Equality." *Rutgers News*. Created 29 February 2016. https://news.rutgers.edu/feature/ruth-bader-ginsburg-former-rutgers-law-professor-led

-legal-campaign-gender-equality/20160228#.XPLCRNNKjOR (Accessed 31 May 2019).

36. ". . . focused legal mind."—Rafei, Roya. "Ruth Bader Ginsburg: The Former Rutgers Law Professor Led the Legal Campaign for Gender Equality." *Rutgers News.* Created 29 February 2016. https://news.rutgers .edu/feature/ruth-bader-ginsburg-former-rutgers-law-professor-led -legal-campaign-gender-equality/20160228#.XPLCRNNKjOR (Accessed 31 May 2019).

37. ". . . written thus far."—Ginsburg, Ruth Bader; Hartnett, Mary; Williams, Wendy W. *My Own Words.* Pg. 113. New York: Simon & Schuster, 2016.

38. ". . . put up with them."—Hirsham, Linda. *Sisters in Law.* Pg. 25. New York: HarperCollins, 2015.

39. ". . . feminism ideology."—De Hart, Jane Sherron. *Ruth Bader Ginsburg.* Pg. 119. New York: Alfred A. Knopf, Penguin Random House, 2018.

40. ". . . not thought of before."—De Hart, Jane Sherron. *Ruth Bader Ginsburg.* Pg. 119. New York: Alfred A. Knopf, Penguin Random House, 2018.

41. ". . . out loud to her daughter."—De Hart, Jane Sherron. *Ruth Bader Ginsburg.* Pg. 119. New York: Alfred A. Knopf, Penguin Random House, 2018.

42. ". . . advance the movement."—Rafei, Roya. "Ruth Bader Ginsburg: The Former Rutgers Law Professor Led the Legal Campaign for Gender Equality." *Rutgers News.* Created 29 February 2016. https: //news.rutgers.edu/feature/ruth-bader-ginsburg-former-rutgers -law-professor-led-legal-campaign-gender-equality/20160228# .XPLCRNNKjOR (Accessed 31 May 2019).

43. ". . . women working."—De Hart, Jane Sherron. *Ruth Bader Ginsburg.* Pg. 163. New York: Alfred A. Knopf, Penguin Random House, 2018.

44. ". . . roles in society."—De Hart, Jane Sherron. *Ruth Bader Ginsburg.* Pg. 152. New York: Alfred A. Knopf, Penguin Random House, 2018.

45. ". . . episode of Radiolab."—Longoria, Julia, "Sex Appeal,". *Radiolab.* Created 23 November 2017. Transcript online. https://www.wnyc studios.org/story/sex-appeal (Accessed 10 May 2019).

46. ". . . so what's the issue."—De Hart, Jane Sherron. *Ruth Bader Ginsburg.* Pg. 169. New York: Alfred A. Knopf, Penguin Random House, 2018.

47. "... legislatures and courts."—Ginsburg, Ruth Bader. "Advocating the Elimination of Gender-Based Discrimination." *Iowa State University Archives of Women's Political Communication.* Created 10 February 2006. https://awpc.cattcenter.iastate.edu/2017/03/09/advocating-the -elimination-of-gender-based-discrimination-feb-10-2006/ (Accessed 18 June 2019).

48. "... but in a cage."—"Advocating the Elimination of Gender-Based Discrimination." Iowa State University Archives of Women's Political Communication. Created 10 February 2006. https://awpc.cattcenter .iastate.edu/2017/03/09/advocating-the-elimination-of-gender-based-discrimination-feb-10-2006/ (Accessed 18 June 2019).

49. "... women's rights cause."—"ACLU History: A Driving Force for Change: The ACLU Women's Rights Project." https://www.aclu .org/other/aclu-history-driving-force-change-aclu-womens-rights-project (Accessed 31 May 2019).

50. "ability to be free." "... women's rights cause."—"ACLU History: A Driving Force for Change: The ACLU Women's Rights Project." https://www.aclu.org/other/aclu-history-driving-force-change-aclu-womens-rights-project (Accessed 31 May 2019).

51. "... during the 1970s." ACLU. *Timeline of Major Supreme Court Decisions on Women's Rights.* https://www.aclu.org/other/timeline-major-supreme-court-decisions-womens-rights (Accessed 10 May 2019).

52. "... near and dear."—Campbell, Amy Leigh. "Raising the Bar: Ruth Bader Ginsburg and the ACLU Women's Rights Project." *Texas Journal of Women and the Law.* 11, p. 221. Created 20 March 2003.

53. "... actually good for women."—Longoria, Julia, "Sex Appeal." *Radiolab.* Created 23 November 2017. Full transcript available online. https://www.wnycstudios.org/story/sex-appeal (Accessed May 10, 2019).

54. "... like a Trojan horse."—Longoria, Julia, "Sex Appeal.". *Radiolab.* Created 23 November 2017. Full transcript available online. https://www.wnycstudios.org/story/sex-appeal (Accessed 10 May 2019).

55. "... unspoken idea" and "... courtrooms or political office."— Longoria, Julia, "Sex Appeal." *Radiolab.* Created 23 November 2017. Full transcript available online. https://www.wnycstudios.org/story/sex-appeal (Accessed 10 May 2019).

56. ". . . for all sexes."—Hirsham, Linda. *Sisters in Law*. Pg. 64. New York: HarperCollins, 2015.

57. ". . . two o'clock class."—De Hart, Jane Sherron. *Ruth Bader Ginsburg*. Pg. 248. New York: Alfred A. Knopf, Penguin Random House, 2018.

58. ". . . anywhere could have."—Ginsburg, Ruth Bader. "Ruth Bader Ginsburg's Advice for Living," the *New York Times*. Created 1 October 2016. https://www.nytimes.com/2016/10/02/opinion/sunday/ruth-bader-ginsburgs-advice-for-living.html (Accessed 1 June 2019).

59. *Weinberger v. Wiesenfeld* case information. "Weinberger v. Wiesenfeld." Oyez. https://www.oyez.org/cases/1974/73–1892 (Accessed June 20, 2019).

60. ". . . wrote the *Washington Post*."—Barnes, Robert, "Ginsburg Performs Wedding for Man in 1970s Case She Argued Before the Supreme Court," *Washington Post*. Created 25 May 2014. https://www.washingtonpost.com/politics/ginsburg-performs-wedding-for-man-in-1970s-case-she-argued-before-the-supreme-court/2014/05/25/a1add474-e114-11e3-9743-bb9b59cde7b9_story.html?utm_term=.1641c2c9e67d (Accessed 9 May 2019).

61. ". . . issue of *The Record*."—Sherr, Lynn. *The Record, Vol. 56, No. 1*. Created Winter 2001. https://www2.nycbar.org/Publications/record/winter01.1.pdf (Accessed 9 May 2019).

62. ". . . Columbia Law School."—Hirsham, Linda. *Sisters in Law*. Pg. 213. New York: HarperCollins, 2015.

63. ". . . too would pass."—Hirsham, Linda. *Sisters in Law*. Pg. 245. New York: HarperCollins, 2015.

64. Info on both Weisenfeld weddings.—Barnes, Robert, "Ginsburg Performs Wedding for Man in 1970s Case She Argued Before the Supreme Court," *Washington Post*. Created 25 May 2014. https://www.washingtonpost.com/politics/ginsburg-performs-wedding-for-man-in-1970s-case-she-argued-before-the-supreme-court/2014/05/25/a1add474-e114-11e3-9743-bb9b59cde7b9_story.html?utm_term=.1641c2c9e67d (Accessed 9 May 2019).

65. Quote about cert petition and ". . . coming down the pipeline."—University of Michigan. "5 Former Clerks Share Thoughts About Justice Ginsburg." *Law Quadrangle*. Created 2 February 2015. https://quadrangle.law.umich.edu/spring2015/umichlaw/5-former-clerks-share-thoughts-about-justice-ginsburg/ (Accessed 31 May 2019).

66. ". . . cautious crusader," and ". . . firmly in focus."—University of Michigan. "5 Former Clerks Share Thoughts About Justice Ginsburg." *Law Quadrangle.* Created 2 February 2015. https://quadrangle.law.umich.edu/spring2015/umichlaw/5-former-clerks-share-thoughts-about-justice-ginsburg/ (Accessed 31 May 2019).

67. ". . . fifteen times."—Williams, Joan. "Beyond the Tough Guise: Justice Ginsburg's Reconstructive Feminism." Pg. 60 in *The Legacy of Ruth Bader Ginsburg,* ed. Scott Dodson. (New York: Cambridge University Press, 2015).

68. ". . . reconstructing gender."—Williams, Joan C. "Reconstructive Feminism: Changing the Way We Talk About Gender and Work Thirty Years After the PDA," *Yale Journal of Law and Feminism* 21. (2009). Pg. 91. https://digitalcommons.law.yale.edu/yjlf/vol21/iss1/5 (Accessed 19 June 2019).

69. ". . . and vice versa."—Williams, Joan C. "Reconstructive Feminism: Changing the Way We Talk About Gender and Work Thirty Years After the PDA," 21 Yale J.L. & Feminism (2009). Pg. 91. https://digitalcommons.law.yale.edu/yjlf/vol21/iss1/5 (Accessed 19 June 2019).

70. Struck Case.—Siegel, Neil S. and Siegel, Reva B. "*Struck* by Stereotype: Ruth Bader Ginsburg on Pregnancy Discrimination as Sex Discrimination." Pg. 776. *Duke Law Journal.* https://scholarship.law.duke.edu/cgi/viewcontent.cgi?referer=&httpsredir=1&article=1450&context=dlj (Accessed 31 May 2019).

71. ". . . imposed upon them."—Siegel, Neil S. and Siegel, Reva B. "*Struck* by Stereotype: Ruth Bader Ginsburg on Pregnancy Discrimination as Sex Discrimination." Pg. 781. *Duke Law Journal.* https://scholarship.law.duke.edu/cgi/viewcontent.cgi?referer=&httpsredir=1&article=1450&context=dlj (Accessed 31 May 2019).

72. ". . . lower status than men."—Siegel, Neil S. and Siegel, Reva B. "*Struck* by Stereotype: Ruth Bader Ginsburg on Pregnancy Discrimination as Sex Discrimination." Pg. 781. *Duke Law Journal.* https://scholarship.law.duke.edu/cgi/viewcontent.cgi?referer=&httpsredir=1&article=1450&context=dlj (Accessed 31 May 2019).

73. ". . . women equal opportunity."—Siegel, Neil S. and Siegel, Reva B. "*Struck* by Stereotype: Ruth Bader Ginsburg on Pregnancy Discrimination as Sex Discrimination." Pg. 798. *Duke Law Journal.* https://scholarship.law.duke.edu/cgi/viewcontent.cgi?referer=&httpsredir=1&article=1450&context=dlj (Accessed 31 May 2019).

74. ". . . this line of thinking."—Williams, Joan. "Beyond the Tough Guise: Justice Ginsburg's Reconstructive Feminism." Pg. 56 in *The Legacy of Ruth Bader Ginsburg*, ed. Scott Dodson. (New York: Cambridge University Press, 2015).

75. ". . . instead hurt, women."—Ginsburg, Ruth Bader; Hartnett, Mary; Williams, Wendy W. *My Own Words*. Pg. 133–136. New York: Simon & Schuster, 2016.

76. Number of briefs and arguments and ". . . Thurgood Marshall of the women's movement."—Ginsburg, Ruth Bader; Hartnett, Mary; Williams, Wendy W. *My Own Words*. Pg. 116. New York: Simon & Schuster, 2016.

77. ". . . 114-year history."—Oelsner, Lesley. "Ruth Bader Ginsburg discussing her post at Columbia." *New York Times*. Created 26 January 1972. https://www.nytimes.com/1972/01/26/archives /columbia-law-snares-a-prize-in-the-quest-for-women-professors .html (Accessed 19 June 2019).

78. ". . . male janitors."—Carmon, Irin, and Knizhnik, Shana. "That time when the Notorious RBG saved the jobs of two dozen maids at Columbia." *Splinter*. Created 3 November 2015. https://splinter news.com/that-time-when-the-notorious-rbg-saved-the-jobs-of -two-1793852519 (Accessed 31 May 2019).

79. ". . . reputation at the school was."—Carmon, Irin, and Knizhnik, Shana. "That time when the Notorious RBG saved the jobs of two dozen maids at Columbia." *Splinter*. Created 3 November 2015. https://splinternews.com/that-time-when-the-notorious-rbg-saved -the-jobs-of-two-1793852519 (Accessed 31 May 2019).

80. Info about how many briefs and time on DC Circuit—Ginsburg, Ruth Bader; Hartnett, Mary; Williams, Wendy W. *My Own Words*. Pg. 116. New York: Simon & Schuster, 2016.

81. ". . . nearly 200 opinions."—Blakemore, Erin, "Ruth Bader Ginsburg's Landmark Opinions on Women's Rights." Website of the History Channel. Created 9 November 2018. https://www.history .com/news/ruth-bader-ginsburgs-landmark-opinions-womens- rights-supreme-court (Accessed May 9, 2019).

82. ". . . in the 1970s."—Ginsburg, Ruth Bader; Hartnett, Mary; Williams, Wendy W. *My Own Words*. Pg. 116. New York: Simon & Schuster, 2016.

83. ". . . men serving on the bench."—"Ginsburg Wants to See All-Female Supreme Court." *CBS Local.* Created 27 November 2012. https://washington.cbslocal.com/2012/11/27/ginsburg-wants-to-see -all-female-supreme-court/ (Accessed 20 June 2019).

84. ". . . sheer pleasure," and "spare," and ". . . tightly reasoned."— Hubbard, Shanti. *2005 Annual Report,* ACLU Women's Rights Project. Created December 2005.

85. ". . . justice's editing style."—Carmon, Irin, and Knizhnik, Shana. *Notorious RBG: The Life and Times of Ruth Bader Ginsburg.* Pg. 122. New York: HarperCollins, 2015.

86. Sam Bagenstos quotes.—University of Michigan. "5 Former Clerks Share Thoughts About Justice Ginsburg." *Law Quadrangle.* Created 2 February 2015. https://quadrangle.law.umich.edu/spring2015/ umichlaw/5-former-clerks-share-thoughts-about-justice-ginsburg/ (Accessed 31 May 2019).

Chapter 2: On Equality for All

1. ". . . afford was a fur coat."—Karbo, Karen. "Ruth Bader Ginsburg on the power of 'difficult women.'" *National Geographic.* Created 9 November 2018. https://www.nationalgeographic.com/culture /2018/11/ruth-bader-ginsburg-in-praise-of-difficult-women-book/ (Accessed 31 May 2019).

2. ". . . outside the building."—De Hart, Jane Sherron. *Ruth Bader Ginsburg.* Pg. 325. New York: Alfred A. Knopf, Penguin Random House, 2018.

3. ". . . shalt thou pursue."—Boorstein, Michelle. "Ruth Bader Ginsburg calls for equal rights amendment to the Constitution." *Washington Post.* Created 2 February 2018. https://www .washingtonpost.com/news/acts-of-faith/wp/2018/02/02/carrying -an-i-dissent-tote-bag-on-stage-ruth-bader-ginsburg-tells-d-c-crowd -shes-still-going-full-steam/?utm_term=.74d1133c48b7 (Accessed 19 June 2019).

4. ". . . as Jane De Hart writes."—De Hart, Jane Sherron. *Ruth Bader Ginsburg.* Pg. 534. New York: Alfred A. Knopf, Penguin Random House, 2018.

5. ". . . that they follow."—Couric, Katie. "Ruth Bader Ginsburg on Trump, Kaepernick and her lifelong love of the law." *Yahoo News.* Created 10 October 2016. https://news.yahoo.com/ruth-bader

-ginsburg-on-trump-kaepernick-and-her-lifelong-love-of-the -law-132236633.html (Accessed 31 May 2019).

6. ". . . no dogs or Jews allowed."—Ginsburg, Ruth Bader; Hartnett, Mary; Williams, Wendy W. *My Own Words*. Pg. 6. New York: Simon & Schuster, 2016.

7. ". . . celebrating their differences."—Ginsburg, Ruth Bader; Hartnett, Mary; Williams, Wendy W. *My Own Words*. Pg. 275. New York: Simon & Schuster, 2016.

8. ". . . country and world."—Lapidus, Lenor M.; Luthra, Namita; and Martin, Emily. "Celebrating Thirty Years: Women's Rights Project Annual Report 2001." *ACLU*. Pg. 9. Created December 2001.

9. ". . . authors of *Notorious RBG*."—Carmon, Irin, and Knizhnik, Shana. *Notorious RBG: The Life and Times of Ruth Bader Ginsburg*. Pg. 33. New York: Harper Collins, 2015.

10. ". . . license would do."—Carmon, Irin, and Knizhnik, Shana. *Notorious RBG: The Life and Times of Ruth Bader Ginsburg*. Pg. 33. New York: Harper Collins, 2015.

11. ". . . citizenship stature."—De Hart, Jane Sherron. *Ruth Bader Ginsburg*. Pg. 534. New York: Alfred A. Knopf, Penguin Random House, 2018.

12. ". . . power of the government."—Griffin, Lisa Kern. "Barriers to Entry and Justice Ginsburg's Criminal Procedure Jurisprudence" in *The Legacy of Ruth Bader Ginsburg*, ed. Scott Dodson. Pg. 104. (New York: Cambridge University Press, 2015), 102–116.

13. ". . . to preserve the remnants."—Griffin, Lisa Kern. "Barriers to Entry and Justice Ginsburg's Criminal Procedure Jurisprudence" in *The Legacy of Ruth Bader Ginsburg*, ed. Scott Dodson. Pg. 104. (New York: Cambridge University Press, 2015), 102–116.

14. ". . . access to justice."—Hirsham, Linda. *Sisters in Law*. Pg. 279. New York: HarperCollins, 2015.

15. ". . . access to court."—Griffin, Lisa Kern. "Barriers to Entry and Justice Ginsburg's Criminal Procedure Jurisprudence" in *The Legacy of Ruth Bader Ginsburg*, ed. Scott Dodson. Pg. 106. (New York: Cambridge University Press, 2015), 102–116.

16. ". . . by the government."—Griffin, Lisa Kern. "Barriers to Entry and Justice Ginsburg's Criminal Procedure Jurisprudence" in *The Legacy of Ruth Bader Ginsburg*, ed. Scott Dodson. Pg. 115. (New York: Cambridge University Press, 2015), 102–116.

17. "...interview with *The New Yorker*."—Toobin, Jeffrey. "Heavyweight: How Ruth Bader Ginsburg has moved the Supreme Court." *The New Yorker*. Created 11 March 2013. https://www.newyorker.com/magazine/2013/03/11/heavyweight-ruth-bader-ginsburg (Accessed 31 May 2019).

18. ". . . continue to evolve."—Toobin, Jeffrey. "Heavyweight: How Ruth Bader Ginsburg has moved the Supreme Court." *The New Yorker*. Created 11 March 2013. https://www.newyorker.com/magazine/2013/03/11/heavyweight-ruth-bader-ginsburg (Accessed 31 May 2019).

19. ". . . defendant ended up there."—Griffin, Lisa Kern. "Barriers to Entry and Justice Ginsburg's Criminal Procedure Jurisprudence" in *The Legacy of Ruth Bader Ginsburg*, ed. Scott Dodson. Pg. 106. (New York: Cambridge University Press, 2015), 102–116.

20. ". . . past injustices."—Griffin, Lisa Kern. "Barriers to Entry and Justice Ginsburg's Criminal Procedure Jurisprudence" in *The Legacy of Ruth Bader Ginsburg*, ed. Scott Dodson. Pg. 106. (New York: Cambridge University Press, 2015), 102–116.

21. ". . . and a fair jury."—Griffin, Lisa Kern. "Barriers to Entry and Justice Ginsburg's Criminal Procedure Jurisprudence" in *The Legacy of Ruth Bader Ginsburg*, ed. Scott Dodson. Pg. 106. (New York: Cambridge University Press, 2015), 102–116.

22. ". . . fair and equal."—Griffin, Lisa Kern. "Barriers to Entry and Justice Ginsburg's Criminal Procedure Jurisprudence" in *The Legacy of Ruth Bader Ginsburg*, ed. Scott Dodson. Pg. 106. (New York: Cambridge University Press, 2015), 102–116.

23. History on *Loving v. Virginia*.—Ginsburg, Ruth Bader; Hartnett, Mary; Williams, Wendy W. *My Own Words*. Pg. 265. New York: Simon & Schuster, 2016.

24. ". . . US Supreme Court."—Ginsburg, Ruth Bader; Hartnett, Mary; Williams, Wendy W. *My Own Words*. Pg. 265. New York: Simon & Schuster, 2016.

25. ". . . we have come as a country."—Ginsburg, Ruth Bader; Hartnett, Mary; Williams, Wendy W. *My Own Words*. Pg. 267. New York: Simon & Schuster, 2016.

26. ". . . equal rights for all."—De Hart, Jane Sherron. *Ruth Bader Ginsburg*. Pg. 534. New York: Alfred A. Knopf, Penguin Random House, 2018.

27. ". . . racially and gender diverse."—Askin, Frank. "Why Only Justice Ginsburg Got Affirmative Action Right." *The Huffington Post.* Created 17 July 2013. https://www.huffpost.com/entry/ruth-bader-ginsburg -affirmative-action_b_3611613 (Accessed 31 May 2019).

28. ". . . sections of people."—Ginsburg, Ruth Bader; Hartnett, Mary; Williams, Wendy W. *My Own Words.* Pg. 269. New York: Simon & Schuster, 2016.

29. Facts of *Fisher v. University of Texas*—Ginsburg, Ruth Bader; Hartnett, Mary; Williams, Wendy W. *My Own Words.* Pg. 296. New York: Simon & Schuster, 2016.

30. ". . . need for the UT program."—Epps, Garrett. "Is Affirmative Action Finished?" *The Atlantic.* Created 10 December 2015. https: //www.theatlantic.com/politics/archive/2015/12/when-can-race-be -a-college-admissions-factor/419808/#Correction1 (Accessed 2 June 2019).

31. ". . . of the court of appeals."—Schwartz, John. "Between the Lines of the Affirmative Action Opinion." *New York Times.* Created 24 June 2013. https://archive.nytimes.com/www.nytimes.com/interactive /2013/06/24/us/annotated-supreme-court-decision-on-affirmative -action.html?module=inline (Accessed 2 June 2019).

32. ". . . upheld the program at UT."—Liptak, Adam. "Supreme Court Upholds Affirmative Action Program at University of Texas." *New York Times.* https://www.nytimes.com/2016/06/24/us/politics/supreme -court-affirmative-action-university-of-texas.html (Accessed 2 June 2019).

33. ". . . you are not getting wet."—"Shelby County v. Holder." Oyez, www.oyez.org/cases/2012/12–96. (Accessed 20 June 2019).

34. ". . . on the Supreme Court."—Butler, Paul. "Ruth Bader Ginsburg can learn something from Brett Kavanaugh." *Washington Post.* Created 15 October 2018. https://www.washingtonpost.com/opinions/ruth -b a d e r - g i n s b u r g - c a n - l e a r n - s o m e t h i n g - f r o m - b r e t t - k a vanaugh/2018/10/15/b8974a86-cd77-11e8-a360-85875bac0b1f _story.html?utm_term=.f4c21e742116 (Accessed 13 May 2019).

35. ". . . Columbia Circuit."—Butler, Paul. "Ruth Bader Ginsburg can learn something from Brett Kavanaugh." *Washington Post.* Created 15 October 2018. https://www.washingtonpost.com/opinions /ruth-bader-ginsburg-can-learn-something-from-brett-ka

vanaugh/2018/10/15/b8974a86-cd77-11e8-a360-85875bac0b1f
_story.html?utm_term=.f4c21e742116 (Accessed 13 May 2019).

36. ". . . clerks were nonwhite."—Butler, Paul. "Ruth Bader Ginsburg can learn something from Brett Kavanaugh." *Washington Post.* Created 15 October 2018. https://www.washingtonpost.com /opinions/ruth-bader-ginsburg-can-learn-something-from-brett-ka vanaugh/2018/10/15/b8974a86-cd77-11e8-a360-85875bac0b1f _story.html?utm_term=.f4c21e742116 (Accessed 13 May 2019).

37. ". . . pushes back," and ". . . 10 more years," and ". . . remarkable career."—Butler, Paul, "Ruth Bader Ginsburg can learn something from Brett Kavanaugh." *Washington Post.* Created 15 October 2018. https://www.washingtonpost.com/opinions/ruth-bader-ginsburg-can-learn -something-from-brett-kavanaugh/2018/10/15 /b8974a86-cd77-11e8-a360-85875bac0b1f_story.html?utm_term =.f4c21e742116 (Accessed May 31, 2019).

38. ". . . world a reality."—Berman, Paul Schiff. "Ruth Bader Ginsburg and the Interaction of Legal Systems" in *The Legacy of Ruth Bader Ginsburg,* ed. Scott Dodson. Pg. 152. (New York: Cambridge University Press, 2015), 151–172.

39. ". . . all the world's people."—Ginsburg, Ruth Bader. ""A Decent Respect to the Opinions of [Human]kind: The Value of a Comparative Perspective in Constitutional Adjudication." Supreme Court Public Information. Created 7 February 2006. https://www.supremecourt .gov/publicinfo/speeches/sp_02-07b-06.html (Accessed 18 June 2019).

40. ". . . courts as well—Ginsburg, Ruth Bader. "A decent Respect to the Opinions of [Human]kind: The Value of a Comparative Perspective in Constitutional Adjudication." Supreme Court Public Information. 30 July 2010. https://www.supremecourt.gov/publicinfo/speeches/ viewspeech/sp_08-02-10 (Accessed 21 June 2019).

41. Paragraph about Eva Moberg and *Stockholm Daily* column.—Gluck, Abbe R. and Metzger, Gillian, "A Conversation with Justice Ruth Bader Ginsburg" (2013). Faculty Scholarship Series. 4905. https: //digitalcommons.law.yale.edu/fss_papers/4905

42. ". . . figure out what was best."—Ginsburg, Ruth Bader; Hartnett, Mary; Williams, Wendy W. *My Own Words.* Pg. 250. New York: Simon & Schuster, 2016.

43. ". . . basic rights for their people?"—Berman, Paul Schiff. "Ruth Bader Ginsburg and the Interaction of Legal Systems" in *The Legacy of Ruth*

Bader Ginsburg, ed. Scott Dodson. Pg. 164. (New York: Cambridge University Press, 2015), 151–172.

44. "... from their efforts."—Ginsburg, Ruth Bader; Hartnett, Mary; Williams, Wendy W. *My Own Words.* Pg. 253. New York: Simon & Schuster, 2016.

45. "... *Reynolds v. United States.*"—Bravin, Jess. "Looking Global: Ginsburg Speaks Out on Kagan, Comparative Law Issue." *The Wall Street Journal.* Created 30 July 2010. https://blogs.wsj.com /law/2010/07/30/looking-global-ginsburg-speaks-out-on-kagan -comparative-law-issue/ (Accessed 31 May 2019).

46. "... we should avoid."—Bravin, Jess. "Looking Global: Ginsburg Speaks Out on Kagan, Comparative Law Issue." *Wall Street Journal.* Created 30 July 2010. https://blogs.wsj.com/law/2010/07/30/look-ing-global-ginsburg-speaks-out-on-kagan-comparative-law-issue/ (Accessed 31 May 2019).

47. "... are pondering."—Bravin, Jess. "Looking Global: Ginsburg Speaks Out on Kagan, Comparative Law Issue." *Wall Street Journal.* Created 30 July 2010. https://blogs.wsj.com/law/2010/07/30/looking-global-ginsburg-speaks-out-on-kagan-comparative-law-issue/ (Accessed 31 May 2019).

48. "... US is facing."—Ginsburg, Ruth Bader; Hartnett, Mary; Williams, Wendy W. *My Own Words.* Pg. 255. New York: Simon & Schuster, 2016.

49. "... Ruth Bader Ginsburg."—Berman, Paul Schiff. "Ruth Bader Ginsburg and the Interaction of Legal Systems" in *The Legacy of Ruth Bader Ginsburg,* ed. Scott Dodson. Pg. 165. (New York: Cambridge University Press, 2015), 151–172.

50. "... not just her words."—Totenberg, Nina. "Notes on a Life" in *The Legacy of Ruth Bader Ginsburg,* ed. Scott Dodson. Pg. 8. (New York: Cambridge University Press, 2015), 3–12.

51. "... sex-based discrimination."—Kumar, Naveen. "*On the Basis of Sex:* Why the Protections RBG Fought for Might Be in Jeopardy." *them.* Created 24 December 2018. https://www.them.us/story /on-the-basis-of-sex-rbg (Accessed 21 June 2019).

52. "... tied to one's sex."—Kumar, Naveen. "*On the Basis of Sex:* Why the Protections RBG Fought for Might Be in Jeopardy." *them.* Created 24 December 2018. https://www.them.us/story/on-the-basis -of-sex-rbg (Accessed 21 June 2019).

53. ". . . Ginsburg helped set."—Ford, Zack. "LGBTQ people are still fighting for protection 'on the basis of sex.'" *ThinkProgress.* Created 12 January 2019. https://thinkprogress.org/lgbtq-ginsburg-on-the -basis-of-sex-00d5c6b2279a/ (Accessed 21 June 2019).

54. ". . . their right to marry."—Ford, Zack. "LGBTQ people are still fighting for protection 'on the basis of sex.'" *ThinkProgress.* Created 12 January 2019. https://thinkprogress.org/lgbtq-ginsburg-on-the -basis-of-sex-00d5c6b2279a/ (Accessed 21 June 2019).

55. ". . . in 2013."—Hurley, Lawrence. "U.S. Supreme Court Justice Ginsburg to preside over gay wedding." Reuters. Created 30 August 2013. https://www.reuters.com/article/us-usa-court-gaymarriage /u-s-supreme-court-justice-ginsburg-to-preside-over-gay-wedding -idUSBRE97T10820130830 (Accessed 13 May 2019).

56. ". . . way it once was?"—Richards, Kimberley. "Five of Ruth Bader Ginsburg's historic moments as she marks 25 years as Supreme Court Justice." *The Independent.* Created 10 August 2018. https: //www.independent.co.uk/news/world/americas/us-politics /ruth-bader-ginsburg-rbg-best-moments-supreme-court-justice-legacy -anniversary-a8487071.html (Accessed 13 May 2019).

57. ". . . LGBT marriages."—Barnes, Robert. "Ginsburg to officiate same-sex wedding." *Washington Post.* Created 30 August 2013. https://www.washingtonpost.com/politics/ginsburg-to-officiate-same -sex-wedding/2013/08/30/4bc09d86-0ff4-11e3-8cdd bcdc09410972_story.html?utm_term=.59b1a7bbe355 (Accessed 13 May 2019).

58. ". . . in the marriage relationship."—Barnes, Robert. "Ginsburg to offi-ciate same-sex wedding." *Washington Post.* Created 30 August 2013. https://www.washingtonpost.com/politics/ginsburg-to-officiate -same-sex-wedding/2013/08/30/4bc09d86-0ff4-11e3-8cdd -bcdc09410972_story.html?utm_term=.59b1a7bbe355 (Accessed 13 May 2019).

59. ". . . who was gay or lesbian."—De Hart, Jane Sherron. *Ruth Bader Ginsburg.* Pg. 468. New York: Alfred A. Knopf, Penguin Random House, 2018.

60. ". . . get it right" and "keep it tight."—Showalter, Elaine. "Fighting Words: Why Ruth Bader Ginsburg is Speaking Out—And What it Means for the Battles Ahead." *New Republic.* Created 3 October

2016. https://newrepublic.com/article/137040/fighting-words (Accessed 19 June 2019).

61. ". . . many years apart."—Griffin, Lisa Kern. "Barriers to Entry and Justice Ginsburg's Criminal Procedure Jurisprudence" in *The Legacy of Ruth Bader Ginsburg,* ed. Scott Dodson. Pg. 108. (New York: Cambridge University Press, 2015), 117–137.

62. ". . . against doing so."—Huq, Aziz, Z. "Justice Ruth Bader Ginsburg and the American Criminal Justice System" in *The Legacy of Ruth Bader Ginsburg,* ed. Scott Dodson. Pg. 117. (New York: Cambridge University Press, 2015), 117–137.

63. ". . . wants and needs." ". . . democratic sentiment."—Huq, Aziz, Z. "Justice Ruth Bader Ginsburg and the American Criminal Justice System" in *The Legacy of Ruth Bader Ginsburg,* ed. Scott Dodson. Pg. 117–18. (New York: Cambridge University Press, 2015), 117–137.

64. ". . . constitutional doctrine."—Hirsham, Linda. *Sisters in Law.* Pg. 26. New York: HarperCollins, 2015.

Part II: The Importance of Relationships

1. Quote about Marty.—Ginsburg, Ruth Bader. "Ruth Bader Ginsburg's Advice for Living." Created 1 October 2016. https://www.nytimes.com/2016/10/02/opinion/sunday/ruth-bader-ginsburgs-advice-for-living.html (Accessed 1 June 2019).

2. Quote about collegiality.—Kliff, Sarah. "It helps to sometimes be a little deaf": A great piece of advice from Ruth Bader Ginsburg." *Vox.* Created 2 October 2016. https://www.vox.com/2016/10/2/13137832/ruth-bader-ginsburg-advice (Accessed 31 May 2019).

Chapter 3: On Marrying Somebody Like Marty

1. Marty cheating and "safe" company.—De Hart, Jane Sherron. *Ruth Bader Ginsburg.* Pg. 41. New York: Alfred A. Knopf, Penguin Random House, 2018.

2. ". . . intellectually and emotionally."—De Hart, Jane Sherron. *Ruth Bader Ginsburg.* Pg. 43. New York: Alfred A. Knopf, Penguin Random House, 2018.

3. ". . . that I had a brain."—Couric, Katie. "Exclusive: Ruth Bader Ginsburg on Hobby Lobby Dissent." *Yahoo News.* Created 30 July

2014. https://news.yahoo.com/katie-couric-interviews-ruth-bader -ginsburg-185027624.html (Accessed 19 May 2019).

4. ". . . glib," and "dead air time," and story about RBG thinking— Ginsburg, Ruth Bader; Hartnett, Mary; Williams, Wendy W. *My Own Words*. Pg. 25. New York: Simon & Schuster, 2016.

5. ". . . before."—Ginsburg, Ruth Bader; Hartnett, Mary; Williams, Wendy W. *My Own Words*. Pg. 26. New York: Simon & Schuster, 2016.

6. ". . . was in it."—Ginsburg, Ruth Bader; Hartnett, Mary; Williams, Wendy W. *My Own Words*. Pg. 26. New York: Simon & Schuster, 2016.

7. ". . . were inseparable."—De Hart, Jane Sherron. *Ruth Bader Ginsburg*. Pg. 43. New York: Alfred A. Knopf, Penguin Random House, 2018.

8. ". . . parent's Long Island home."—Ginsburg, Ruth Bader; Hartnett, Mary; Williams, Wendy W. *My Own Words*. Time line in front of book (Pg. 1–2). New York: Simon & Schuster, 2016.

9. ". . . little deaf sometimes" and earplugs. Shapiro, T. Rees, "Martin D. Ginsburg dies at 78," *Washington Post*. Created 28 June 2010. http:// www.washingtonpost.com/wp-dyn/content/article/2010/06/27/ AR2010062703220.html?tid=a_inl_manual (Accessed 22 April 2019)

10. ". . . both her marriage, and on the court." Sullivan, Kathleen J, "U.S. Supreme Court Justice Ginsburg talks about a meaningful life."*Stanford News*. Created 6 February 2017. https://news.stanford .edu/2017/02/06/supreme-court-associate-justice-ginsburg-talks- meaningful-life/ (Accessed 23 April 2019).

11. ". . . and a willingness to share domestic duties."—Shapiro, T. Rees, "Martin D. Ginsburg dies at 78," *Washington Post*. Created 28 June 2010. http://www.washingtonpost.com/wp-dyn/content/ article/2010/06/27/AR2010062703220.html?tid=a_inl_manual (Accessed 22 April 2019)

12. ". . . for his generation," and ". . . choice unreservedly."—Nomination of Ruth Bader Ginsburg, to be Associate Justice of the Supreme Court of the United States. *Committee on the Judiciary*. Pg. 50. Washington: US Government Printing Office, 1994. https://www.loc.gov/law /find/nominations/ginsburg/hearing.pdf (Accessed 19 June 2019).

13. ". . . marrying Marty."—Ginsburg, Ruth Bader; Hartnett, Mary; Williams, Wendy W. *My Own Words*. Pg. 26. New York: Simon & Schuster, 2016.

14. Info on their post marriage life.—Ginsburg, Ruth Bader; Hartnett, Mary; Williams, Wendy W. *My Own Words*. Pg. xviii. New York: Simon & Schuster, 2016.

15. ". . . find a way to do it."—Ginsburg, James. "Martin and Ruth Bader Ginsburg: A Thoroughly Modern Love Story (Guest Column)." *The Hollywood Reporter*. Created 14 February 2019. https://www.holly woodreporter.com/news/martin-ruth-bader-ginsburg-a-thoroughly -modern-love-story-guest-column-1186442 (Accessed 31 May 2019).

16. ". . . head back to school early" and Ruth going to Sweden—De Hart, Jane Sherron. *Ruth Bader Ginsburg*. Pg. 66, Pg. 86. New York: Alfred A. Knopf, Penguin Random House, 2018.

17. Info on their life.—Shapiro, T. Rees, "Martin D. Ginsburg dies at 78," *Washington Post*. Created 28 June 2010. http://www.washingtonpost .com/wp-dyn/content/article/2010/06/27/AR2010062703220.html ?tid=a_inl_manual (Accessed 22 April 2019)

18. ". . . chances of his survival were 'almost nil.'"—Totenberg, Nina. "Notes on a Life" in *The Legacy of Ruth Bader Ginsburg*, ed. Scott Dodson. (New York: Cambridge University Press, 2015), 3–12.

19. ". . . that semester."—De Hart, Jane Sherron. *Ruth Bader Ginsburg*. Pg. 71. New York: Alfred A. Knopf, Penguin Random House, 2018.

20. ". . . what life is."—"Ruth Bader Ginsburg on the Perspective that Comes with Motherhood." *The Atlantic*. Created 6 February 2017. https://www.theatlantic.com/video/index/515631/ruth-bader -ginsburg-motherhood/ (Accessed 31 May 2019).

21. ". . . respite from the other."—"Ruth Bader Ginsburg on the Perspective that Comes with Motherhood." *The Atlantic*. Created 6 February 2017. https://www.theatlantic.com/video/index/515631 /ruth-bader-ginsburg-motherhood/ (Accessed 31 May 2019).

22. ". . . at her side."—Tunney, Kelly. "Ruth Bader Ginsburg Has Relationship Advice to Help Any Couple Make It." *Bustle*. Created 3 October 2016. https://www.bustle.com/articles/187492-ruth -bader-ginsburg-has-relationship-advice-to-help-any-couple -make-it (Accessed 19 June 2019).

23. Section on Marty bringing Ruth a tax brief.—Ginsburg, Ruth Bader; Hartnett, Mary; Williams, Wendy W. *My Own Words*. Pg. 128. New York: Simon & Schuster, 2016.

24. ". . . highest bench in the land."—Ginsburg, Ruth Bader; Hartnett, Mary; Williams, Wendy W. *My Own Words*. Pg. 129. New York: Simon & Schuster, 2016.

25. ". . . when she speaks in public."—Carmon, Irin, and Knizhnik, Shana. *Notorious RBG: The Life and Times of Ruth Bader Ginsburg*. Pg. 44. New York: Harper Collins, 2015.

26. ". . . campaign manager."—Izadi, Elahe. *Washington Post*. Created 31 July 2014. https://www.washingtonpost.com/news/post-nation/wp/2014/07/31/ruth-bader-ginsburgs-advice-on-love-and-leaning-in/?utm_term=.434d46cf196e (Accessed 22 April 2019).

27. ". . . DC judge."—De Hart, Jane Sherron. *Ruth Bader Ginsburg*. Pg. 317. New York: Alfred A. Knopf, Penguin Random House, 2018.

28. ". . . press attention."—Izadi, Elahe. *Washington Post*. Created 31 July 2014. https://www.washingtonpost.com/news/post-nation/wp/2014/07/31/ruth-bader-ginsburgs-advice-on-love-and-leaning-in/?utm_term=.434d46cf196e (Accessed 22 April 2019).

29. ". . . betray no secret."—Tunney, Kelly. "Ruth Bader Ginsburg Has Relationship Advice to Help Any Couple Make It." *Bustle*. Created 03 October 2016. https://www.bustle.com/articles/187492-ruth-bader-ginsburg-has-relationship-advice-to-help-any-couple-make-it (Accessed 19 June 2019).

30. White House counsel Ron Klain quote.—Ginsburg, Ruth Bader; Hartnett, Mary; Williams, Wendy W. *My Own Words*. Pg. *xix*. New York: Simon & Schuster, 2016.

31. ". . . voiced the question."—Katzmann, Robert. "Reflections on the Confirmation Journey of Ruth Bader Ginsburg, Summer 1993." in *The Legacy of Ruth Bader Ginsburg*, ed. Scott Dodson. Pg. 201. (New York: Cambridge University Press, 2015), 199–205.

32. ". . . always worth following."—Katzmann, Robert. "Reflections on the Confirmation Journey of Ruth Bader Ginsburg, Summer 1993." in *The Legacy of Ruth Bader Ginsburg*, ed. Scott Dodson. Pg. 201. (New York: Cambridge University Press, 2015), 199–205.

33. ". . . Marty had made."—Katzmann, Robert. "Reflections on the Confirmation Journey of Ruth Bader Ginsburg, Summer 1993." in

The Legacy of Ruth Bader Ginsburg, ed. Scott Dodson. Pg. 201. (New York: Cambridge University Press, 2015), 199–205.

34. ". . . slept, sometimes."—Carmon, Irin, and Knizhnik, Shana. *Notorious RBG: The Life and Times of Ruth Bader Ginsburg.* Pg. 99. New York: Harper Collins, 2015.

35. ". . . best baguette."—Williams, Joan C., and Ginsburg, Ruth Bader. "Conversation with Justice Ginsburg." C-SPAN. Created 15 September 2011. https://www.c-span.org/video/?301560–1/conversation-justice-ginsburg (Accessed 31 May 2019).

36. ". . . started over again."—Williams, Joan C., and Ginsburg, Ruth Bader. "Conversation with Justice Ginsburg." C-SPAN. Created 15 September 2011. https://www.c-span.org/video/?301560–1/conversation-justice-ginsburg (Accessed 31 May 2019).

37. "vegetable until she was 14," and ". . . by her children."—Carmon, Irin, and Knizhnik, Shana. *Notorious RBG: The Life and Times of Ruth Bader Ginsburg.* Pg. 100. New York: Harper Collins, 2015.

38. ". . . doing all the cooking."—Carmon, Irin, and Knizhnik, Shana. *Notorious RBG: The Life and Times of Ruth Bader Ginsburg.* Pg. 100. New York: Harper Collins, 2015.

39. ". . . chef supreme."—Toobin, Jeffrey. "Heavyweight: How Ruth Bader Ginsburg has moved the Supreme Court." *The New Yorker.* Created 11 March 2013. https://www.newyorker.com/magazine/2013/03/11/heavyweight-ruth-bader-ginsburg (Accessed May 31, 2019).

40. ". . . 50 steps long."—Toobin, Jeffrey and Harlow, Poppy. "Dissenter" in *RBG: Beyond Notorious.* CNN. Created 20 August 2018. https://podcasts.apple.com/us/podcast/rbg-beyond-notorious/id1424366161 (Accessed 31 May 2019).

41. ". . . cooking dad!"—Schulman, Michael. "Ruth Bader Ginsburg's Nephew on Winning the Aunt Lottery." *The New Yorker.* Created 17 December 2013. https://www.newyorker.com/magazine/2018/12/24/ruth-bader-ginsburgs-nephew-on-winning-the-aunt-lottery (Accessed 31 May 2019).

42. "posture, tidiness, or diet."—De Hart, Jane Sherron. *Ruth Bader Ginsburg.* Pg. 97. New York: Alfred A. Knopf, Penguin Random House, 2018.

43. ". . . was him."—De Hart, Jane Sherron. *Ruth Bader Ginsburg.* Pg. 299. New York: Alfred A. Knopf, Penguin Random House, 2018.

44. ". . . once said."—Williams, Joan C., and Ginsburg, Ruth Bader. "Conversation with Justice Ginsburg." C-SPAN. Created 15 September 2011. https://www.c-span.org/video/?301560–1/conversation-justice -ginsburg (Accessed 31 May 2019).

45. ". . . in Ruth's life."—Couric, Katie. "Exclusive: Ruth Bader Ginsburg on Hobby Lobby Dissent." *Yahoo News.* Created 30 July 2014. https://news.yahoo.com/katie-couric-interviews-ruth-bader -ginsburg-185027624.html (Accessed May 19, 2019).

46. ". . . loved ones."—Ginsburg, James. "Martin and Ruth Bader Ginsburg: A Thoroughly Modern Love Story (Guest Column)." *Hollywood Reporter.* Created 14 February 2019. https://www.holly woodreporter.com/news/martin-ruth-bader-ginsburg-a-thoroughly-modern-love-story-guest-column-1186442 (Accessed 31 May 2019).

47. ". . . follow her."—Ginsburg, James. "Martin and Ruth Bader Ginsburg: A Thoroughly Modern Love Story (Guest Column)." *The Hollywood Reporter.* Created 14 February 2019. https://www.holly woodreporter.com/news/martin-ruth-bader-ginsburg-a-thoroughly -modern-love-story-guest-column-1186442 (Accessed 31 May 2019).

48. ". . . it's family."—Shapiro, T. Rees. *Washington Post.* Created 28 June 2010. http://www.washingtonpost.com/wp-dyn/content/article /2010/06/27/AR2010062703220.html?tid=a_inl_manual (Accessed 22 April 2019).

49. ". . . book The Notorious RBG."—Carmon, Irin and Knizhnik, Shana. *Notorious RBG: The Life and Times of Ruth Bader Ginsburg.* Pg. 105. New York: Harper Collins, 2015.

50. Story Heather Elliott gave for reunion.—Carmon, Irin, and Knizhnik, Shana. *Notorious RBG: The Life and Times of Ruth Bader Ginsburg.* Pg. 105. New York: Harper Collins, 2015.

51. ". . . stomach pumped."—"Ruth Bader Ginsburg on the Perspective that Comes with Motherhood." *The Atlantic.* Created 6 February 2017. https://www.theatlantic.com/video/index/515631/ruth-bader -ginsburg-motherhood/ (Accessed 31 May 2019).

52. ". . . nearest hospital."—De Hart, Jane Sherron. *Ruth Bader Ginsburg.* Pg. 98. New York: Alfred A. Knopf, Penguin Random House, 2018.

53. ". . . burns on his face."—De Hart, Jane Sherron. *Ruth Bader Ginsburg.* Pg. 98. New York: Alfred A. Knopf, Penguin Random House, 2018.

54. ". . . according to Jane Ginsburg."—De Hart, Jane Sherron. *Ruth Bader Ginsburg*. Pg. 98. New York: Alfred A. Knopf, Penguin Random House, 2018.

55. ". . . taken it?"—Totenberg, Nina. "Justice Ruth Bader Ginsburg's Life Immortalized in Song." NPR. 18 July 2018. https://www.npr.org/2018/07/18/623893240/justice-ruth-bader-ginsburgs-life-immortalized-in-song (Accessed 19 June 2019).

56. ". . . almost every one."—Ginsburg, James. "Martin and Ruth Bader Ginsburg: A Thoroughly Modern Love Story (Guest Column)." *Hollywood Reporter*. Created 14 February 2019. https://www.hollywoodreporter.com/news/martin-ruth-bader-ginsburg-a-thoroughly-modern-love-story-guest-column-1186442 (Accessed 31 May 2019).

57. ". . . deadpanned with a laugh."—Gibian, Rebecca. "'The Notorious RBG' draws sold-out audience in New York." The Associated Press. Created 15 December 2018. https://www.apnews.com/b52177e39004491aa68048eb10aef1c3 (Accessed 31 May 2019).

58. ". . . Her Highness."—Toobin, Jeffrey. "Heavyweight: How Ruth Bader Ginsburg has moved the Supreme Court." *The New Yorker*. Created 11 March 2013. https://www.newyorker.com/magazine/2013/03/11/heavyweight-ruth-bader-ginsburg (Accessed 31 May 2019).

59. ". . . as well as these guys."—Carmon, Irin, and Knizhnik, Shana. *Notorious RBG: The Life and Times of Ruth Bader Ginsburg*. Pg. 99. New York: Harper Collins, 2015.

60. ". . . more to be done."—Toobin, Jeffrey. "Heavyweight: How Ruth Bader Ginsburg has moved the Supreme Court." *The New Yorker*. Created 11 March 2013. https://www.newyorker.com/magazine/2013/03/11/heavyweight-ruth-bader-ginsburg (Accessed 31 May 2019).

61. ". . . yellow pad."—Totenberg, Nina. "No, Ruth Bader Ginsburg Does Not Intend to Retire Anytime Soon." 90.9 WBUR. Created 3 October 2016. https://www.wbur.org/npr/495820477/no-ruth-bader-ginsburg-does-not-intend-to-retire-anytime-soon (Accessed 18 June 2019).

62. Marty's note.—Totenberg, Nina, and Ginsburg, Ruth Bader. "Ruth Bader Ginsburg: Justice for All." *What It Takes*. Begins at 53:30, ends 55:35. Created 26 September 2016. https://whatittakes.simplecast.com/episodes/40ca4a6b-40ca4a6b (Accessed 18 June 2019).

63. ". . . her cry."—Totenberg, Nina. "No, Ruth Bader Ginsburg Does Not Intend to Retire Anytime Soon." 90.9 WBUR. Created 3 October 2016. https://www.wbur.org/npr/495820477/no-ruth -bader-ginsburg-does-not-intend-to-retire-anytime-soon (Accessed 18 June 2019).

64. ". . . enable Ruth to do what she has done."—Totenberg, Nina. "Notes on a Life" in *The Legacy of Ruth Bader Ginsburg,* ed. Scott Dodson. Pg. 6. (New York: Cambridge University Press, 2015), 3–12.

Chapter 4: On Building and Maintaining Relationships

1. ". . . mouth them instead."—Ginsburg, Ruth Bader. "Prefaces to Scalia/Ginsburg: A (Gentle) Parody of Operatic Proportions." *Columbia Journal of Law & The Arts.* Created 2015. https://lawandarts .org/article/prefaces-to-scaliaginsburg-a-gentle-parody-of-operatic-proportions/ (Accessed May 14, 2019).

2. ". . . also wanted to be a diva."—Ginsburg, Ruth Bader; Hartnett, Mary; Williams, Wendy W. *My Own Words.* Pg. 44. New York: Simon & Schuster, 2016.

3. ". . . of Justice Scalia."—Fang, Marina. "Ruth Bader Ginsburg Remembers Antonin Scalia, Her Dear Friend and Sparring Partner." *Huffington Post.* Created 14 February 2016. https://www .huffpost.com/entry/scalia-ginsburg-friendship_n_56bfb717e4b 0b40245c6f436 (Accessed 19 June 2019).

4. ". . . just clicked."—Toobin, Jeffrey and Harlow, Poppy. "The Odd Couple" in *RBG: Beyond Notorious.* 7:38. CNN. Created 22 August 2018. https://podcasts.apple.com/us/podcast/rbg-beyond-notorious /id1424366161 (Accessed 31 May 2019).

5. ". . . Marty would cook it."—Toobin, Jeffrey and Harlow, Poppy. "The Odd Couple" in *RBG: Beyond Notorious.* 9:38 to 9:50. CNN. Created 22 August 2018. https://podcasts.apple.com/us/podcast /rbg-beyond-notorious/id1424366161 (Accessed 31 May 2019).

6. Roses and shopper.—Ginsburg, Ruth Bader; Hartnett, Mary; Williams, Wendy W. *My Own Words.* Pg. 39–42. New York: Simon & Schuster, 2016.

7. ". . . friendships with them."—Toobin, Jeffrey. "Heavyweight: How Ruth Bader Ginsburg has moved the Supreme Court." *The New Yorker.* Created 11 March 2013. https://www.newyorker.com/magazine

/2013/03/11/heavyweight-ruth-bader-ginsburg (Accessed 31 May 2019).

8. ". . . more conservative colleagues."—De Hart, Jane Sherron. *Ruth Bader Ginsburg.* Pg. 139. New York: Alfred A. Knopf, Penguin Random House, 2018.

9. ". . . intellectually with him."—Toobin, Jeffrey and Harlow, Poppy. "The Odd Couple" in *RBG: Beyond Notorious.* 13:24. CNN. Created 22 August 2018. https://podcasts.apple.com/us/podcast/rbg -beyond-notorious/id1424366161 (Accessed 31 May 2019).

10. ". . . infectious."—Zimmerman, Amy. "Supreme Court Justice Ruth Bader Ginsburg Fact-Checks Her Own Biopic, 'On the Basis of Sex.'" *The Daily Beast.* Created 18 December 2018. https://www.thedaily beast.com/supreme-court-justice-ruth-bader-ginsburg-fact-checks -her-own-biopic-on-the-basis-of-sex (Accessed 31 May 2019).

11. ". . . after Scalia's death."—Zimmerman, Amy. "Supreme Court Justice Ruth Bader Ginsburg Fact-Checks Her Own Biopic, 'On the Basis of Sex.'" *The Daily Beast.* Created 18 December 2018. https: //www.thedailybeast.com/supreme-court-justice-ruth-bader-ginsburg -fact-checks-her-own-biopic-on-the-basis-of-sex (Accessed 31 May 2019).

12. ". . . as best we can."—Ginsburg, Ruth Bader. "Lighter Side of Life at the United States Supreme Court." *New England Law | Boston.* Created 13 March 2009. https://www.supremecourt.gov/publicinfo /speeches/viewspeech/sp_03-13-09 (Accessed 18 June 2019).

13. ". . . avoid making it personal," and ". . . bolstered their friend-ship."—Toobin, Jeffrey and Harlow, Poppy. "The Odd Couple" in *RBG: Beyond Notorious.* 13:16 to 13:32. CNN. Created 22 August 2018. https://podcasts.apple.com/us/podcast/rbg-beyond-notorious /id1424366161 (Accessed 31 May 2019).

14. ". . . that they serve."—Fang, Marina. "Ruth Bader Ginsburg Remembers Antonin Scalia, Her Dear Friend and Sparring Partner." *The Huffington Post.* Created 14 February 2016. https://www .huffpost.com/entry/scalia-ginsburg-friendship_n_56bfb717e4b 0b40245c6f436 (Accessed 19 June 2019).

15. ". . . assigned to them."—Ginsburg, Ruth Bader; Hartnett, Mary; Williams, Wendy W. *My Own Words.* Pg. 37. New York: Simon & Schuster, 2016.

16. ". . . not strong friendships."—Toobin, Jeffrey and Harlow, Poppy. "The Odd Couple" in *RBG: Beyond Notorious*. 18:38 to 19:15. CNN. Created 22 August 2018. https://podcasts.apple.com/us/podcast /rbg-beyond-notorious/id1424366161 (Accessed 31 May 2019).

17. ". . . tomorrow is another day."—Remarks by Ruth Bader Ginsburg at "A Special Tribute to Justice Sandra Day O'Connor" as part of Seneca Women Global Leadership Forum. Created 15 April 2015. 1:25 to 1:45 in video. https://www.senecawomen.com/tribute-to-justice-sandradayoconnor (Accessed 19 June 2019).

18. ". . . besides Justice John Paul Stevens."—Carmon, Irin, and Knizhnik, Shana. *Notorious RBG: The Life and Times of Ruth Bader Ginsburg*. Pg. 113. New York: Harper Collins, 2015.

19. ". . . on all the courts below."—Hirsham, Linda. *Sisters in Law*. Pg. 222. New York: HarperCollins, 2015.

20. ". . . while on the court."—Hirsham, Linda. *Sisters in Law*. Pg. 253–54. New York: HarperCollins, 2015.

21. ". . . session on Monday."—Hirsham, Linda. *Sisters in Law*. Pg. 253–54. New York: HarperCollins, 2015.

22. ". . . through that hard time."—Williams, Joan C., and Ginsburg, Ruth Bader. "Conversation with Justice Ginsburg." C-SPAN. Created 15 September 2011. https://www.c-span.org/video/?301560–1 /conversation-justice-ginsburg (Accessed 31 May 2019).

23. ". . . my first days and weeks."—Remarks by Ruth Bader Ginsburg at "A Special Tribute to Justice Sandra Day O'Connor" as part of Seneca Women Global Leadership Forum. Created 15 April 2015. Quote found 3:40 to 4:18 in video. https://www.senecawomen.com/ tribute-to-justice-sandradayoconnor (Accessed 19 June 2019).

24. ". . . strenuous case."—Ginsburg, Ruth Bader; Hartnett, Mary; Williams, Wendy W. *My Own Words*. Pg. 90. New York: Simon & Schuster, 2016.

25. ". . . anger or resentment."—Ginsburg, Ruth Bader; Hartnett, Mary; Williams, Wendy W. *My Own Words*. Pg. 90. New York: Simon & Schuster, 2016.

26. ". . . Spera said."—Spera, Clara. "Ruth Bader Ginsburg's Granddaughter: 'You Know Her as the Notorious RBG, but She's Bubbie to Me.'" *Glamour*. Created 4 May 2018. https://www .glamour.com/story/ruth-bader-ginsburg-granddaughter-bubbie -to-me (Accessed 31 May 2019).

27. ". . . their own egos."—McCarthy, Erin. "15 Memorable Ruth Bader Ginsburg Quotes." *MentalFloss*. Created 15 March 2019. http://mentalfloss.com/article/62023/15-awesome-ruth-bader-ginsburg-quotes-her-84th-birthday (Accessed 21 June 2019).

28. "...founddiningtogether."—SupremeCourtProject.C-SPAN.Created 20 December 2010. https://www.c-span.org/video/?297213–1/the-supreme-court-home-americas-highest-court-2010-edition&start=5 (Accessed 14 May 2019).

29. ". . . dinner for all the justices."—Ginsburg, Ruth Bader; Hartnett, Mary; Williams, Wendy W. *My Own Words*. Pg. 57. New York: Simon & Schuster, 2016.

30. ". . . three times a year."—Carmon, Irin, and Knizhnik, Shana. *Notorious RBG: The Life and Times of Ruth Bader Ginsburg*. Pg. 104. New York: Harper Collins, 2015.

31. ". . . is or should be."—Ginsburg, Ruth Bader; Hartnett, Mary; Williams, Wendy W. *My Own Words*. Pg. 213. New York: Simon & Schuster, 2016.

32. ". . . conservatives finding dates."—Schwartz, Drew. "Conservatives Are Whining Because No One Wants to Date Them." *VICE*. Created 5 March 2018. https://www.vice.com/en_us/article/gy893x/conservatives-are-whining-because-no-one-wants-to-date-them-vgtrn (Accessed 14 May 2019).

33. ". . . to strengthen them."—de Vogue, Ariane. "At VMI, Ruth Bader Ginsburg Reflects on a Monumental Ruling." CNN. Created 13 August 2018. https://www.cnn.com/2017/02/02/politics/ruth-bader-ginsburg-vmi/index.html (Accessed 21 June 2019).

34. ". . . respond to it in her opinion."—de Vogue, Ariane. "At VMI, Ruth Bader Ginsburg Reflects on a Monumental Ruling." CNN. Created 13 August 2018. https://www.cnn.com/2017/02/02/politics/ruth-bader-ginsburg-vmi/index.html (Accessed 21 June 2019).

35. ". . . very clear."—Hill, Herma Kay. "Ruth Bader Ginsburg: Law Professor Extraordinaire" in *The Legacy of Ruth Bader Ginsburg*, ed. Scott Dodson. Pg. 29. (New York: Cambridge University Press, 2015), 12–30.

36. ". . . future cases."—Hill, Herma Kay. "Ruth Bader Ginsburg: Law Professor Extraordinaire" in *The Legacy of Ruth Bader Ginsburg*, ed. Scott Dodson. Pg. 29. (New York: Cambridge University Press, 2015), 12–30.

37. ". . . articulated opinions."—Hill, Herma Kay. "Ruth Bader Ginsburg: Law Professor Extraordinaire" in *The Legacy of Ruth Bader Ginsburg,* ed. Scott Dodson. Pg. 30. (New York: Cambridge University Press, 2015), 12–30.

38. ". . . deftness and grace," and ". . . good partner," and ". . . take breaks"—Park, Ryan. "What Ruth Bader Ginsburg Taught Me About Being a Stay-at-Home Dad." *The Atlantic.* Created 8 January 2015. https://www.theatlantic.com/business/archive/2015/01/what-ruth -bader-ginsburg-taught-me-about-being-a-stay-at-home-dad /384289/ (Accessed 31 May 2019).

39. ". . . cheer her up."—Totenberg, Nina. "Notes on a Life" in *The Legacy of Ruth Bader Ginsburg,* ed. Scott Dodson. Pg. 10. (New York: Cambridge University Press, 2015), 3–12.

40. ". . . wonderful boss."—University of Michigan. "5 Former Clerks Share Thoughts About Justice Ginsburg." *Law Quadrangle.* Created 2 February 2015. https://quadrangle.law.umich.edu/spring2015 /umichlaw/5-former-clerks-share-thoughts-about-justice-ginsburg/ (Accessed 31 May 2019).

41. ". . . day one of clerking for her."—University of Michigan. "5 Former Clerks Share Thoughts About Justice Ginsburg." *Law Quadrangle.* Created 2 February 2015. https://quadrangle.law.umich.edu /spring2015/umichlaw/5-former-clerks-share-thoughts-about-justice -ginsburg/ (Accessed 31 May 2019).

42. ". . . chambers along with her."—University of Michigan. "5 Former Clerks Share Thoughts About Justice Ginsburg." *Law Quadrangle.* Created 2 February 2015. https://quadrangle.law.umich.edu /spring2015/umichlaw/5-former-clerks-share-thoughts-about-justice -ginsburg/ (Accessed 31 May 2019).

43. ". . . anything else."—Toobin, Jeffrey. "Heavyweight: How Ruth Bader Ginsburg has moved the Supreme Court." *The New Yorker.* Created 11 March 2013. https://www.newyorker.com/magazine /2013/03/11/heavyweight-ruth-bader-ginsburg (Accessed 31 May 2019).

Chapter 5: On the Shoulders We Stand On

1. ". . . women, she said."—Carmon, Irin, and Knizhnik, Shana. *Notorious RBG: The Life and Times of Ruth Bader Ginsburg.* Pg. 119. New York: Harper Collins, 2015.

2. Story about Sonia Sotomayor dancing.—Biskupic, Joan. *Breaking In: The Rise of Sonia Sotomayor and the Politics of Justice.* Pg. 6. New York: Sarah Crichton Books, 2014.

3. ". . . women should be considered equal."—Ryzik, Melena. "Bringing to Life the Ruth Bader Ginsburg Only Her Family Knows." *New York Times.* Created 27 December 2018. https://www.nytimes .com/2018/12/27/movies/on-the-basis-of-sex-ruth-bader-ginsburg .html (Accessed 17 May 2019).

4. ". . . during an interview in 2018."—Ryzik, Melena. "Bringing to Life the Ruth Bader Ginsburg Only Her Family Knows." *New York Times.* Created 27 December 2018. https://www.nytimes .com/2018/12/27/movies/on-the-basis-of-sex-ruth-bader-ginsburg .html (Accessed 17 May 2019).

5. ". . . into the script."—Ryzik, Melena. "Bringing to Life the Ruth Bader Ginsburg Only Her Family Knows." *New York Times.* Created 27 December 2018. https://www.nytimes.com/2018/12/27/movies /on-the-basis-of-sex-ruth-bader-ginsburg.html (Accessed 17 May 2019).

6. ". . . way paver or pathmaker."—Ginsburg, Ruth Bader; Hartnett, Mary; Williams, Wendy W. *My Own Words.* Pg. 63. New York: Simon & Schuster, 2016.

7. ". . . Ginsburg herself did."—Ginsburg, Ruth Bader; Hartnett, Mary; Williams, Wendy W. *My Own Words.* Pg. 63. New York: Simon & Schuster, 2016.

8. *Reed v. Reed* brief and info on Kenyon and Murray.—Kerber, Linda K. "Before *Frontiero* There Was *Reed*: Ruth Badeer Ginsburg and the Constitutional Transformation of the Twentieth Century" in *The Legacy of Ruth Bader Ginsburg*, ed. Scott Dodson. Pg. 43. (New York: Cambridge University Press, 2015), 44–56.

9. ". . . years before."—Kerber, Linda K. "Before *Frontiero* There Was *Reed*: Ruth Bader Ginsburg and the Constitutional Transformation of the Twentieth Century" in *The Legacy of Ruth Bader Ginsburg*, ed. Scott Dodson. Pg. 43. (New York: Cambridge University Press, 2015), 44–56.

10. ". . . distracting associations."—Crocker, Catherine. "Ginsburg Explains Origin of Sex, Gender: Justice: Supreme Court's newest member speaks at her old law school and brings down the house with her history lesson about fighting bias." *Los Angeles Times.*

Created 21 November 1993. https://www.latimes.com/archives /la-xpm-1993-11-21-mn-59217-story.html (Accessed 31 May 2019).

11. ". . . great ladies"—Ginsburg, Ruth Bader. "Women in the Federal Judiciary: Three Way Pavers and the Exhilarating Change President Carter Wrought." *Fordham Law Review.* Created 1995. https: //ir.lawnet.fordham.edu/flr/vol64/iss2/1/ (Accessed 17 May 2019).

12. ". . . life in the law."—Ginsburg, Ruth Bader. "Women in the Federal Judiciary: Three Way Pavers and the Exhilarating Change President Carter Wrought." *Fordham Law Review.* Created 1995. https://ir .lawnet.fordham.edu/flr/vol64/iss2/1/ (Accessed 17 May 2019

13. ". . . in the majority."—Ginsburg, Ruth Bader; Hartnett, Mary; Williams, Wendy W. *My Own Words.* Pg. 65. New York: Simon & Schuster, 2016.

14. ". . . for president."—Ginsburg, Ruth Bader; Hartnett, Mary; Williams, Wendy W. *My Own Words.* Pg. 65. New York: Simon & Schuster, 2016.

15. ". . . the invisible seen."—Lithwick, Dahlia. "Notorious Ruth Bader Ginsburg as a precise, white-gloved wonk." *Washington Post.* Created 20 October 2016. https://www.washingtonpost.com/opinions /notorious-ruth-bader-ginsburg-as-a-precise-white-gloved -wonk/2016/10/20/b9e2ab0a-949f-11e6-bb29-bf2701dbe0a3 _story.html?utm_term=.d692bd2265b9 (Accessed 17 May 2019).

16. ". . . but not her mother."—Lithwick, Dahlia. "Notorious Ruth Bader Ginsburg as a precise, white-gloved wonk." *Washington Post.* Created 20 October 2016. https://www.washingtonpost.com /opinions/notorious-ruth-bader-ginsburg-as-a-precise-white-gloved -wonk/2016/10/20/b9e2ab0a-949f-11e6-bb29-bf2701dbe0a3 _story.html?utm_term=.d692bd2265b9 (Accessed 17 May 2019).

17. ". . . few would listen."—Nomination of Ruth Bader Ginsburg, to be Associate Justice of the Supreme Court of the United States. *Committee on the Judiciary.* Pg. 50. Washington: US Government Printing Office, 1994. https://www.loc.gov/law/find/nominations /ginsburg/hearing.pdf (Accessed 19 June 2019).

18. ". . . these brave people."—Nomination of Ruth Bader Ginsburg, to be Associate Justice of the Supreme Court of the United States. *Committee on the Judiciary.* Pg. 50. Washington: US Government Printing Office, 1994. https://www.loc.gov/law/find/nominations /ginsburg/hearing.pdf (Accessed 19 June 2019).

19. ". . . inspiration from it."—Nomination of Ruth Bader Ginsburg, to be Associate Justice of the Supreme Court of the United States. *Committee on the Judiciary.* Pg. 50. Washington: US Government Printing Office, 1994. https://www.loc.gov/law/find/nominations /ginsburg/hearing.pdf (Accessed 19 June 2019).

20. ". . . as much as sons."—Nomination of Ruth Bader Ginsburg, to be Associate Justice of the Supreme Court of the United States. *Committee on the Judiciary.* Pg. 50. Washington: US Government Printing Office, 1994. https://www.loc.gov/law/find/nominations /ginsburg/hearing.pdf (Accessed 19 June 2019).

21. ". . . O'Connor set."—Ginsburg, Ruth Bader; Hartnett, Mary; Williams, Wendy W. *My Own Words.* Pg. 91. New York: Simon & Schuster, 2016.

22. ". . . many more."—Ginsburg, Ruth Bader; Hartnett, Mary; Williams, Wendy W. *My Own Words.* Pg. 91. New York: Simon & Schuster, 2016.

23. ". . . should be Ruth's."—Hirsham, Linda. *Sisters in Law.* Pg. 241. New York: HarperCollins, 2015.

24. ". . . sex discrimination."—Hirsham, Linda. *Sisters in Law.* Pg. 242. New York: HarperCollins, 2015.

25. ". . . women can make."—Hirsham, Linda. *Sisters in Law.* Pg. 233. New York: HarperCollins, 2015.

26. ". . . better off for it."—Remarks by Ruth Bader Ginsburg at "A Special Tribute to Justice Sandra Day O'Connor" as part of Seneca Women Global Leadership Forum. Created 15 April 2015. Quote found 7:50 to 8:20 in video. https://www.senecawomen.com/tribute-to-justice-sandradayoconnor (Accessed 19 June 2019).

27. Story about time with Sandra and T-shirts—Ginsburg, Ruth Bader; Hartnett, Mary; Williams, Wendy W. *My Own Words.* Pg. 92. New York: Simon & Schuster, 2016.

28. ". . . would happen again."—Hirsham, Linda. *Sisters in Law.* Pg. 270. New York: HarperCollins, 2015.

29. ". . . male colleagues lack."—Hirsham, Linda. *Sisters in Law.* Pg. 270. New York: HarperCollins, 2015.

30. ". . . until she was gone."—Hirsham, Linda. *Sisters in Law.* Pg. 270. New York: HarperCollins, 2015.

31. "... principles and loyalty."—Katzmann, Robert. "Reflections on the Confirmation Journey of Ruth Bader Ginsburg, Summer 1993." in *The Legacy of Ruth Bader Ginsburg,* ed. Scott Dodson. Pg. 201. (New York: Cambridge University Press, 2015), 199–205.

Part III: On Being Brave and Creating Change

1. "... seen great changes."—Ginsburg, Ruth Bader. "Ruth Bader Ginsburg's Advice for Living." *New York Times.* Created 1 October 2016. https://www.nytimes.com/2016/10/02/opinion/sunday/ruth -bader-ginsburgs-advice-for-living.html (Accessed 19 June 2019).

Chapter 6: On Hardship

1. "... receive a D."—Ginsburg, Ruth Bader; Hartnett, Mary; Williams, Wendy W. *My Own Words.* Pg. 3. New York: Simon & Schuster, 2016.

2. "... cook or sew."—Ginsburg, Ruth Bader; Hartnett, Mary; Williams, Wendy W. *My Own Words.* Pg. 3. New York: Simon & Schuster, 2016.

3. Paragraph about WWII, Pearl Harbor, "victory garden."—Ginsburg, Ruth Bader; Hartnett, Mary; Williams, Wendy W. *My Own Words.* Pg. 6–7. New York: Simon & Schuster, 2016.

4. "... determination and steeliness."—Sanders, Sam and Totenberg, Nina. "How Ruth Bader Ginsburg Became 'Notorious RBG'". *It's Been a Minute with Sam Sanders,* NPR. Created 15 May 2018. https://www.npr.org/templates/transcript/transcript.php?storyId =610185554 (Accessed 18 May 2019).

5. "... independent and self-sufficient."—Ginsburg, Ruth Bader; Hartnett, Mary; Williams, Wendy W. *My Own Words.* Pg. 5. New York: Simon & Schuster, 2016.

6. "... took it to heart."—Ginsburg, Ruth Bader; Hartnett, Mary; Williams, Wendy W. *My Own Words.* Pg. 5. New York: Simon & Schuster, 2016.

7. "... My Day," and "... enrolled in Hebrew school."—De Hart, Jane Sherron. *Ruth Bader Ginsburg.* Pg. 12. New York: Alfred A. Knopf, Penguin Random House, 2018.

8. "... proud of."—De Hart, Jane Sherron. *Ruth Bader Ginsburg.* Pg. xvii New York: Alfred A. Knopf, Penguin Random House, 2018.

9. "... look up to."—De Hart, Jane Sherron. *Ruth Bader Ginsburg.* Pg. 12. New York: Alfred A. Knopf, Penguin Random House, 2018.
10. "... early years."—De Hart, Jane Sherron. *Ruth Bader Ginsburg.* Pg. 4. New York: Alfred A. Knopf, Penguin Random House, 2018.
11. "... being a baton twirler."—Ginsburg, Ruth Bader; Hartnett, Mary; Williams, Wendy W. *My Own Words.* Pg. 19. New York: Simon & Schuster, 2016.
12. "... strongest and bravest."—Nomination of Ruth Bader Ginsburg, to be Associate Justice of the Supreme Court of the United States. *Committee on the Judiciary.* Pg. 50. Washington: US Government Printing Office, 1994. https://www.loc.gov/law/find/nominations/ginsburg/hearing.pdf (Accessed 19 June 2019).
13. ... fourteen months old."—Ginsburg, Ruth Bader; Hartnett, Mary; Williams, Wendy W. *My Own Words.* Pg. 3. New York: Simon & Schuster, 2016.
14. "... took their exams."—Carmon, Irin, and Knizhnik, Shana. *Notorious RBG: The Life and Times of Ruth Bader Ginsburg.* Pg. 35. New York: Harper Collins, 2015.
15. "... her time at Harvard."—Carmon, Irin, and Knizhnik, Shana. *Notorious RBG: The Life and Times of Ruth Bader Ginsburg.* Pg. 35. New York: Harper Collins, 2015.
16. "... best clerks ever."—Carmon, Irin, and Knizhnik, Shana. *Notorious RBG: The Life and Times of Ruth Bader Ginsburg.* Pg. 39. New York: Harper Collins, 2015.
17. "... into the corporate world."—"Ruth Bader Ginsburg: Rejected by the Firm." *Makers.* Created 12 June 2012. https://www.youtube.com/watch?v=ldFUmU-OZ1U (Accessed 19 June 2019).
18. "... multiple times."—De Hart, Jane Sherron. *Ruth Bader Ginsburg.* Pg. 286. New York: Alfred A. Knopf, Penguin Random House, 2018.
19. "... to the court."—Carmon, Irin, and Knizhnik, Shana. *Notorious RBG: The Life and Times of Ruth Bader Ginsburg.* Pg. 89. New York: Harper Collins, 2015.
20. "... women were there to stay."—Carmon, Irin, and Knizhnik, Shana. *Notorious RBG: The Life and Times of Ruth Bader Ginsburg.* Pg. 112. New York: Harper Collins, 2015.
21. "... chemotherapy and radiation treatments."—Berman, Michele R., and Boguski, Mark S. "Ruth Bader Ginsburg v. Cancer." *MedPage*

Today. Created 10 January 2019. https://www.medpagetoday.com/blogs/celebritydiagnosis/77348 (Accessed 18 May 2019).

22. ". . . routine examinations to assure."—Berman, Michele R., and Boguski, Mark S. "Ruth Bader Ginsburg v. Cancer." *MedPage Today.* Created 10 January 2019. https://www.medpagetoday.com/blogs/celebritydiagnosis/77348 (Accessed 18 May 2019).

23. ". . . single day of oral argument."—Barnes, Robert, and Berman, Mark. "Ruth Bader Ginsburg back on bench as Supreme Court resumes hearings." *Washington Post.* Created 19 February 2019. https://www.washingtonpost.com/politics/courts_law/ruth-bader-ginsburg-expected-on-bench-when-supreme-court-resumes-hearings/2019/02/19/b8ab182e-33c8-11e9-854a-7a14d7fec96a_story.html?utm_term=.c5640679268b (Accessed 31 May 2019).

24. ". . . sense of family."—De Hart, Jane Sherron. *Ruth Bader Ginsburg.* Pg. 385. New York: Alfred A. Knopf, Penguin Random House, 2018.

25. ". . . deeply sad."—De Hart, Jane Sherron. *Ruth Bader Ginsburg.* Pg. 385. New York: Alfred A. Knopf, Penguin Random House, 2018.

26. ". . . certain cases."—Stout, David. "Supreme Court Upholds Ban on Abortion Procedure." *New York Times.* Created 18 April 2007. https://www.nytimes.com/2007/04/18/us/18cnd-scotus.html (Accessed 19 June 2019).

27. ". . . by the court."—De Hart, Jane Sherron. *Ruth Bader Ginsburg.* Pg. 392. New York: Alfred A. Knopf, Penguin Random House, 2018.

28. ". . . for granted."—De Hart, Jane Sherron. *Ruth Bader Ginsburg.* Pg. 394. New York: Alfred A. Knopf, Penguin Random House, 2018.

29. ". . . radiation and chemotherapy."—De Hart, Jane Sherron. *Ruth Bader Ginsburg.* Pg. 411. New York: Alfred A. Knopf, Penguin Random House, 2018.

30. ". . . cancer on two fronts" and ". . . resolves depleted."—De Hart, Jane Sherron. *Ruth Bader Ginsburg.* Pg. 411. New York: Alfred A. Knopf, Penguin Random House, 2018.

31. ". . . I will live."—De Hart, Jane Sherron. *Ruth Bader Ginsburg.* Pg. 411. New York: Alfred A. Knopf, Penguin Random House, 2018.

32. ". . . four more."—De Hart, Jane Sherron. *Ruth Bader Ginsburg.* Pg. 414. New York: Alfred A. Knopf, Penguin Random House, 2018.

33. ". . . their wedding anniversary."—De Hart, Jane Sherron. *Ruth Bader Ginsburg.* Pg. 416. New York: Alfred A. Knopf, Penguin Random House, 2018.

34. "... ashen-faced."—De Hart, Jane Sherron. *Ruth Bader Ginsburg*. Pg. 417. New York: Alfred A. Knopf, Penguin Random House, 2018.

35. Quote by Jane Ginsburg.—Carmon, Irin, and Knizhnik, Shana. *Notorious RBG: The Life and Times of Ruth Bader Ginsburg*. Pg. 107. New York: Harper Collins, 2015.

36. "... Jell-O and cottage cheese."—De Hart, Jane Sherron. *Ruth Bader Ginsburg*. Pg. 417. New York: Alfred A. Knopf, Penguin Random House, 2018.

37. ". . . mother officiated."—De Hart, Jane Sherron. *Ruth Bader Ginsburg*. Pg. 418. New York: Alfred A. Knopf, Penguin Random House, 2018.

38. ". . . outgoing personality."—De Hart, Jane Sherron. *Ruth Bader Ginsburg*. Pg. 421. New York: Alfred A. Knopf, Penguin Random House, 2018.

39. "... five days later."—Bravin, Jess. "Justice Ginsburg Undergoes Heart Procedure to Treat Coronary Blockage." *Wall Street Journal.* https://www.wsj.com/articles/justice-ginsburg-undergoes-heart-procedure-to-treat-coronary-blockage-1417016398 (Accessed 21 June 2019).

40. ". . . stories and wit."—De Hart, Jane Sherron. *Ruth Bader Ginsburg*. Pg. 484. New York: Alfred A. Knopf, Penguin Random House, 2018.

41. ". . . nine months."—De Hart, Jane Sherron. *Ruth Bader Ginsburg*. Pg. 485. New York: Alfred A. Knopf, Penguin Random House, 2018.

42. ". . . prior feedback."—De Hart, Jane Sherron. *Ruth Bader Ginsburg*. Pg. 493. New York: Alfred A. Knopf, Penguin Random House, 2018.

43. ". . . country would be like."—Blake, Aaron. "In bashing Donald Trump, some say Ruth Bader Ginsburg just crossed a very important line." Created 11 July 2016. https://www.washingtonpost.com/news/the-fix/wp/2016/07/11/in-bashing-donald-trump-some-say-ruth-bader-ginsburg-just-crossed-a-very-important-line/?utm_term=.eac716730d1e (Accessed 21 June 2019).

44. ". . . should resign."—Biskupic, Joan. "Justice Ruth Bader Ginsburg calls Trump a 'faker,' he says she should resign." CNN. Created 13 July 2016. https://www.cnn.com/2016/07/12/politics/justice-ruth-bader-ginsburg-donald-trump-faker/index.html (Accessed 21 June 2019).

45. Brett Kavanaugh assault accusations, hearing and confirmation—Stolberg, Sheryl Gay, and Fandos, Nicholas. "Brett Kavanaugh and Christine Blasey Ford Duel with Tears and Fury." *New*

York Times. Created 27 September 2018. https://www.nytimes .com/2018/09/27/us/politics/brett-kavanaugh-confirmation-hearings .html (Accessed 31 May 2019).

46. ". . . toward the end of the year."—Totenberg, Nina. "Justice Ruth Bader Ginsburg Undergoes Surgery for Lung Cancer." NPR. Created 21 December 2018. https://www.npr.org/2018/12/21/679065534/ justice-ruth-bader-ginsburg-undergoes-surgery-for-lung-cancer (Accessed 18 May 2019).

47. ". . . ask a question."—Barnes, Robert, and Berman, Mark. "Ruth Bader Ginsburg back on bench as Supreme Court resumes hearings." *Washington Post.* Created 19 February 2019. https://www.washing tonpost.com/politics/courts_law/ruth-bader-ginsburg-expected- on-bench-when-supreme-court-resumes-hearings/2019/02/19 /b8ab182e-33c8-11e9-854a-7a14d7fec96a_story.html?utm_term= .e744dedb9db2 (Accessed 18 May 2019).

48. ". . . is, in fact, dead."—Barnes, Robert, and Berman, Mark. "Ruth Bader Ginsburg back on bench as Supreme Court resumes hearings." *Washington Post.* Created 19 February 2019. https: //www.washingtonpost.com/politics/courts_law/ruth-bader-ginsburg -expected-on-bench-when-supreme-court-resumes-hearings /2019/02/19/b8ab182e-33c8-11e9-854a-7a14d7fec96a_story.html? utm_term=.e744dedb9db2 (Accessed 18 May 2019).

49. ". . . next week."—Carmon, Irin, and Knizhnik, Shana. *Notorious RBG: The Life and Times of Ruth Bader Ginsburg.* Pg. 13. New York: Harper Collins, 2015.

50. ". . . things were rough."—Couric, Katie. "Exclusive: Ruth Bader Ginsburg on Hobby Lobby Dissent." *Yahoo News.* Created 30 July 2014. https://news.yahoo.com/katie-couric-interviews-ruth-bader-gins burg-185027624.html (Accessed 19 May 2019).

51. ". . . all male."—Lithwick, Dahlia. "Fire and Ice: Ruth Bader Ginsburg, the Least Likely Firebrand" in *The Legacy of Ruth Bader Ginsburg,* ed. Scott Dodson. Pg. 229. (New York: Cambridge University Press, 2015), 222–232.

52. ". . . follow behind."—Katzmann, Robert. "Reflections on the Confirmation Journey of Ruth Bader Ginsburg, Summer 1993" in *The Legacy of Ruth Bader Ginsburg,* ed. Scott Dodson. Pg. 204. (New York: Cambridge University Press, 2015), 199–205.

Chapter 7: On Persuasion over Anger

1. ". . . find her voice."—Greenhouse, Linda. "Oral Dissents Give Ginsburg New Voice On Court." *New York Times.* Created 31 May 2007. https://www.nytimes.com/2007/05/31/washington/31scotus .html (Accessed 21 June 2019).

2. ". . . hiding drugs."—Lithwick, Dahlia. "Fire and Ice: Ruth Bader Ginsburg, the Least Likely Firebrand" in *The Legacy of Ruth Bader Ginsburg,* ed. Scott Dodson. Pg. 228. (New York: Cambridge University Press, 2015), 222–232.

3. ". . . I was about to cry."—Lithwick, Dahlia. "Fire and Ice: Ruth Bader Ginsburg, the Least Likely Firebrand" in *The Legacy of Ruth Bader Ginsburg,* ed. Scott Dodson. Pg. 228. (New York: Cambridge University Press, 2015), 222–232.

4. ". . . transferred schools."—Totenberg, Nina. "Supreme Court Hears School Strip Search Case." NPR. Created 21 April 2009. https: //www.npr.org/templates/story/story.php?storyId=103334943 (Accessed 31 May 2009).

5. ". . . questioned Justice Stephen Breyer."—"Safford Unified School District v. Redding." Oyez. https://www.oyez.org/cases/2008/08 –479 (Accessed June 21, 2019).

6. ". . . might explode."—Totenberg, Nina. "Notes on a Life" in *The Legacy of Ruth Bader Ginsburg,* ed. Scott Dodson. Pg. 10. (New York: Cambridge University Press, 2015), 3–12.

7. ". . . flashing with anger"—Totenberg, Nina. "Supreme Court Hears School Strip Search Case." NPR. Created 21 April 2009. https://www .npr.org/templates/story/story.php?storyId=103334943 (Accessed 31 May 2009).

8. "shake out" and ". . . humiliating position."—"Safford Unified School District v. Redding." Oyez. https://www.oyez.org/cases/2008/08 –479 (Accessed June 21, 2019).

9. ". . . dripping with exasperation."—Totenberg, Nina. "Notes on a Life" in *The Legacy of Ruth Bader Ginsburg,* ed. Scott Dodson. Pg. 10. (New York: Cambridge University Press, 2015), 3–12.

10. ". . . girls, do not."—Totenberg, Nina. "Supreme Court Hears School Strip Search Case." NPR. Created 21 April 2009. https://www.npr .org/templates/story/story.php?storyId=103334943 (Accessed 31 May 2009).

11. ". . . things in my underwear."—"Safford Unified School District v. Redding." Oyez. https://www.oyez.org/cases/2008/08–479 (Accessed June 21, 2019).

12. ". . . beyond human experience."—"Safford Unified School District v. Redding." Oyez. https://www.oyez.org/cases/2008/08–479 (Accessed June 21, 2019).

13. "They have never been a 13-year-old girl" and ". . . it is sometimes the outcome."—Biskupic, Joan. "Ginsburg: Court needs another woman." *USA Today.* Created May 2009. https://usatoday30 .usatoday.com/news/washington/judicial/2009-05-05-ruthginsburg _N.htm (Accessed 1 June 2019).

14. ". . . what's the big deal?"—Bazelon, Emily. "The Place of Women on the Court." *New York Times Magazine.* Created 7 July 2009. https://www.nytimes.com/2009/07/12/magazine/12ginsburg-t.html (Accessed 1 June 2019).

15. ". . . that kind of post."—Bazelon, Emily. "The Place of Women on the court." *New York Times Magazine.* Created 7 July 2009. https://www.nytimes.com/2009/07/12/magazine/12ginsburg-t .html (Accessed 1 June 2019).

16. ". . . the Legacy of Ruth Bader Ginsburg."—Lithwick, Dahlia. "Fire and Ice: Ruth Bader Ginsburg, the Least Likely Firebrand" in *The Legacy of Ruth Bader Ginsburg,* ed. Scott Dodson. Pg. 230. (New York: Cambridge University Press, 2015), 222–232.

17. ". . . choking down."—Lithwick, Dahlia. "Fire and Ice: Ruth Bader Ginsburg, the Least Likely Firebrand" in *The Legacy of Ruth Bader Ginsburg,* ed. Scott Dodson. Pg. 230. (New York: Cambridge University Press, 2015), 222–232.

18. ". . . desire was waning."—Lithwick, Dahlia. "Fire and Ice: Ruth Bader Ginsburg, the Least Likely Firebrand" in *The Legacy of Ruth Bader Ginsburg,* ed. Scott Dodson. Pg. 230. (New York: Cambridge University Press, 2015), 222–232.

19. ". . . lead others to join you."—Ginsburg, Ruth Bader. "Ruth Bader Ginsburg's Advice for Living." Created 1 October 2016. https: //www.nytimes.com/2016/10/02/opinion/sunday/ruth-bader -ginsburgs-advice-for-living.html (Accessed 1 June 2019).

20. ". . . logic, not fireworks."—Lithwick, Dahlia. "Fire and Ice: Ruth Bader Ginsburg, the Least Likely Firebrand" in *The Legacy of Ruth*

Bader Ginsburg, ed. Scott Dodson. Pg. 224. (New York: Cambridge University Press, 2015), 222–232.

21. ". . . teach someone."—Crary, David. "Ginsburg questions 1973 abortion ruling's timing." Associated Press. Created 10 February 2012. https://apnews.com/ef166a59c51344948cbd0b5ddcbf740d (Accessed 1 June 2019).

22. ". . . grew up in the 1950s."—Lithwick, Dahlia. "Fire and Ice: Ruth Bader Ginsburg, the Least Likely Firebrand" in *The Legacy of Ruth Bader Ginsburg*, ed. Scott Dodson. Pg. 223. (New York: Cambridge University Press, 2015), 222–232.

23. ". . . all emotions in."—Lithwick, Dahlia. "Fire and Ice: Ruth Bader Ginsburg, the Least Likely Firebrand" in *The Legacy of Ruth Bader Ginsburg*, ed. Scott Dodson. Pg. 223. (New York: Cambridge University Press, 2015), 222–232.

24. ". . . idea, and then respond."—Biskupic, Joan. "Ginsburg: Court needs another woman." *USA Today*. Created May 2009. https://usatoday30.usatoday.com/news/washington/judicial/2009-05-05-ruthginsburg_N.htm (Accessed 1 June 2019).

25. ". . . will focus on the point." Biskupic, Joan. "Ginsburg: Court needs another woman." *USA Today*. Created May 2009. https://usatoday30.usatoday.com/news/washington/judicial/2009-05-05-ruthginsburg_N.htm (Accessed 1 June 2019).

26. ". . . get her to talk."—Lithwick, Dahlia. "Fire and Ice: Ruth Bader Ginsburg, the Least Likely Firebrand" in *The Legacy of Ruth Bader Ginsburg*, ed. Scott Dodson. Pg. 224. (New York: Cambridge University Press, 2015), 222–232.

27. ". . . conscious of etiquette."—Lithwick, Dahlia. "Fire and Ice: Ruth Bader Ginsburg, the Least Likely Firebrand" in *The Legacy of Ruth Bader Ginsburg*, ed. Scott Dodson. Pg. 227. (New York: Cambridge University Press, 2015), 222–232.

28. ". . . get his vote anyway."—Totenberg, Nina. "Notes on a Life" in *The Legacy of Ruth Bader Ginsburg*, ed. Scott Dodson. Pg. 7. (New York: Cambridge University Press, 2015), 3–12.

29. ". . . women's rights."—Hirsham, Linda. *Sisters in Law*. Pg. xxii. New York: HarperCollins, 2015.

30. ". . . all male elite."—Hirsham, Linda. *Sisters in Law*. Pg. xxii. New York: HarperCollins, 2015.

31. ". . . early and vocal opponent" and "legendary antifeminist."—
    Hirsham, Linda. *Sisters in Law*. Pg. xxii. New York: HarperCollins,
    2015.

32. ". . . should be spanked" and ". . . done for decades."—Hirsham,
    Linda. *Sisters in Law*. Pg. xxii. New York: HarperCollins, 2015.

33. ". . . than mouse."—Hirsham, Linda. *Sisters in Law*. Pg. xxiii. New
    York: HarperCollins, 2015.

34. ". . . collegial tone."—Lithwick, Dahlia. "Fire and Ice: Ruth Bader
    Ginsburg, the Least Likely Firebrand" in *The Legacy of Ruth Bader
    Ginsburg*, ed. Scott Dodson. Pg. 225. (New York: Cambridge
    University Press, 2015), 222–232.

35. ". . . in her own life."—Lithwick, Dahlia. "Fire and Ice: Ruth Bader
    Ginsburg, the Least Likely Firebrand" in *The Legacy of Ruth Bader
    Ginsburg*, ed. Scott Dodson. Pg. 231. (New York: Cambridge
    University Press, 2015), 222–232.

36. ". . . slights and slurs" and ". . . no one was listening."—Lithwick,
    Dahlia. "Fire and Ice: Ruth Bader Ginsburg, the Least Likely
    Firebrand" in *The Legacy of Ruth Bader Ginsburg*, ed. Scott Dodson.
    Pg. 230. (New York: Cambridge University Press, 2015), 222–232.

37. ". . . future generations."—Ginsburg, Ruth Bader; Hartnett, Mary;
    Williams, Wendy W. *My Own Words*. Pg. 277. New York: Simon &
    Schuster, 2016.

38. ". . . remained herself."—Lithwick, Dahlia. "Fire and Ice: Ruth
    Bader Ginsburg, the Least Likely Firebrand" in *The Legacy of Ruth
    Bader Ginsburg*, ed. Scott Dodson. Pg. 231. (New York: Cambridge
    University Press, 2015), 222–232.

39. ". . . whispers anymore."—Lithwick, Dahlia. "Fire and Ice: Ruth
    Bader Ginsburg, the Least Likely Firebrand" in *The Legacy of Ruth
    Bader Ginsburg*, ed. Scott Dodson. Pg. 230–1. (New York: Cambridge
    University Press, 2015), 222–232.

40. ". . . marrying the two."—Lithwick, Dahlia. "Fire and Ice: Ruth
    Bader Ginsburg, the Least Likely Firebrand" in *The Legacy of Ruth
    Bader Ginsburg*, ed. Scott Dodson. Pg. 232. (New York: Cambridge
    University Press, 2015), 222–232.

41. ". . . rule-abiding . . . ," and ". . . not despite them."—Lithwick,
    Dahlia. "The Irony of Modern Feminism's Obsession With Ruth
    Bader Ginsburg." *The Atlantic*. Created January/February 2019.

https://www.theatlantic.com/magazine/archive/2019/01/ruth-bader
-ginsburg-feminist-hero/576403/ (Accessed 1 June 2019).

42. ". . . fighting for equality."—Lithwick, Dahlia. "RBG Reveals the
Woman Behind the Memes." *Slate.* Created 30 April 2018. https:
//slate.com/culture/2018/04/rbg-the-new-documentary-reviewed
.html (Accessed 1 June 2019).

43. ". . . disempowering."—Lithwick, Dahlia. "RBG Reveals the Woman
Behind the Memes." *Slate.* Created 30 April 2018. https://slate.com
/culture/2018/04/rbg-the-new-documentary-reviewed.html
(Accessed 1 June 2019).

44. ". . . once wrote."—Lithwick, Dahlia. "RBG Reveals the Woman
Behind the Memes." *Slate.* Created 30 April 2018. https://slate.com
/culture/2018/04/rbg-the-new-documentary-reviewed.html
(Accessed 1 June 2019).

45. ". . . opposite of a firebrand."—Lithwick, Dahlia. "The Irony of
Modern Feminism's Obsession With Ruth Bader Ginsburg." *The
Atlantic.* Created January/February 2019. https://www.theatlantic
.com/magazine/archive/2019/01/ruth-bader-ginsburg-feminist
-hero/576403/ (Accessed 1 June 2019).

46. ". . . we've turned her into."—Lithwick, Dahlia. "The Irony of Modern
Feminism's Obsession With Ruth Bader Ginsburg." *The Atlantic.*
Created January/February 2019. https://www.theatlantic.com
/magazine/archive/2019/01/ruth-bader-ginsburg-feminist
-hero/576403/ (Accessed 1 June 2019).

47. ". . . Jewish ancestors."—Lithwick, Dahlia. "The Irony of Modern
Feminism's Obsession With Ruth Bader Ginsburg." *The Atlantic.*
Created January/February 2019. https://www.theatlantic.com
/magazine/archive/2019/01/ruth-bader-ginsburg-feminist
-hero/576403/ (Accessed 1 June 2019).

48. ". . . by slow advances."—Lithwick, Dahlia. "The Irony of Modern
Feminism's Obsession With Ruth Bader Ginsburg." *The Atlantic.*
Created January/February 2019. https://www.theatlantic.com
/magazine/archive/2019/01/ruth-bader-ginsburg-feminist
-hero/576403/ (Accessed 1 June 2019).

Chapter 8: On Why, and How, to Dissent

1. Lily Ledbetter facts—Toobin, Jeffrey and Harlow, Poppy. "Dissenter"
in *RBG: Beyond Notorious.* CNN. 10:30 to 22:40. Created 20 August

2018. https://podcasts.apple.com/us/podcast/rbg-beyond-notorious /id1424366161 (Accessed 31 May 2019).

2. ". . . dirty, smelly, and hot factory."—Toobin, Jeffrey and Harlow, Poppy. "Dissenter" in *RBG: Beyond Notorious*. CNN. 10:30 to 22:40. Created 20 August 2018. https://podcasts.apple.com/us/podcast /rbg-beyond-notorious/id1424366161 (Accessed 31 May 2019).

3. Lily Ledbetter Case history—Ginsburg, Ruth Bader; Hartnett, Mary; Williams, Wendy W. *My Own Words*. Pg. 284. New York: Simon & Schuster, 2016.

4. ". . . pay discrimination."—Zients, Sasha. "Lilly Ledbetter: RBG's dissent in landmark case still gives me 'chills.'" CNN. Created 22 August 2018. https://www.cnn.com/2018/08/22/politics/rbg-pod cast-lilly-ledbetter-cnntv/index.html (Accessed 19 June 2019).

5. ". . . Court could not."—Ginsburg, Ruth Bader; Hartnett, Mary; Williams, Wendy W. *My Own Words*. Pg. 285. New York: Simon & Schuster, 2016.

6. ". . . discriminatory action."—Gay Stolberg, Sheryl. "Obama Signs Equal-Pay Legislation." *New York Times*. Created 29 January 2009. https://www.nytimes.com/2009/01/30/us/politics/30ledbet ter-web .html (Accessed 19 June 2019.

7. ". . . meant the world to her."—Toobin, Jeffrey and Harlow, Poppy. "Dissenter" in *RBG: Beyond Notorious*. CNN. 10:30 to 22:40. Created 20 August 2018. https://podcasts.apple.com/us/podcast /rbg-beyond-notorious/id1424366161 (Accessed 31 May 2019).

8. ". . . chills and goosebumps."—Zients, Sasha. "Lilly Ledbetter: RBG's dissent in landmark case still gives me 'chills.'" CNN. Created 22 August 2018. https://www.cnn.com/2018/08/22/politics/rbg-pod cast-lilly-ledbetter-cnntv/index.html (Accessed 19 June 2019).

9. ". . . could've heard it."—Toobin, Jeffrey and Harlow, Poppy. "Dissenter" in *RBG: Beyond Notorious*. CNN. 10:30 to 22:40. Created 20 August 2018. https://podcasts.apple.com/us/podcast /rbg-beyond-notorious/id1424366161 (Accessed 31 May 2019).

10. ". . . future age."—Manning-Schaffel, Vivian. "How to dissent like RBG." NBC News. Created 10 June 2018. https://www.nbcnews .com/better/pop-culture/how-dissent-rbg-ncna881316 (Accessed 22 May 2019).

11. ". . . thinking and changing."—Manning-Schaffel, Vivian. "How to dissent like RBG." NBC News. Created 10 June 2018. https://www

.nbcnews.com/better/pop-culture/how-dissent-rbg-ncna881316 (Accessed 22 May 2019).

12. ". . . NBC News."—Manning-Schaffel, Vivian. "How to dissent like RBG." NBC News. Created 10 June 2018. https://www.nbcnews .com/better/pop-culture/how-dissent-rbg-ncna881316 (Accessed 22 May 2019).

13. ". . . excessively liberal."—De Hart, Jane Sherron. *Ruth Bader Ginsburg*. Pg. 281. New York: Alfred A. Knopf, Penguin Random House, 2018.

14. ". . . consensus builder."—Turan, Kenneth. "Beyond the 'Ginsburn': The documentary 'RBG' shows the formidable soft power of Ruth Bader Ginsburg." *Los Angeles Times*. Created 3 May 2018. https://www.latimes.com/entertainment/movies/la-et-mn-rbg-docu mentary-review-20180503-story.html (Accessed 19 June 2019).

15. ". . . from the bench."—Ginsburg, Ruth Bader; Hartnett, Mary; Williams, Wendy W. *My Own Words*. Pg. 276. New York: Simon & Schuster, 2016.

16. ". . . profoundly misguided."—Ginsburg, Ruth Bader; Hartnett, Mary; Williams, Wendy W. *My Own Words*. Pg. 279. New York: Simon & Schuster, 2016.

17. ". . . Linda Greenhouse. "—Greenhouse, Linda. "Oral Dissents Give Ginsburg a New Voice On Court." *New York Times*. Created 31 May 2007. https://www.nytimes.com/2007/05/31/washington/31scotus .html (Accessed May 22, 2019).

18. ". . . found her voice and used it" and "passionate and pointed"—Greenhouse, Linda. "Oral Dissents Give Ginsburg a New Voice On Court." *New York Times*. Created 31 May 2007. https://www .nytimes.com/2007/05/31/washington/31scotus.html (Accessed 22 May 2019).

19. ". . . most frequent bench dissenter."—Ginsburg, Ruth Bader; Hartnett, Mary; Williams, Wendy W. *My Own Words*. Pg. 277. New York: Simon & Schuster, 2016.

20. ". . . nearly three decades."—Ginsburg, Ruth Bader; Hartnett, Mary; Williams, Wendy W. *My Own Words*. Pg. 277. New York: Simon & Schuster, 2016.

21. ". . . composition of the court."—Rosen, Jeffrey. "Ruth Bader Ginsburg is an American Hero." *New Republic*. Created 28 September 2014. https://newrepublic.com/article/119578/ruth-bader-ginsburg-inter view-retirement-feminists-jazzercise (Accessed 1 June 2019).

22. ". . . you're not getting wet."—"Shelby County v. Holder." Oyez, www.oyez.org/cases/2012/12–96. (Accessed 20 June 2019).

23. ". . . by today's decision."—"Shelby County v. Holder." Oyez, www .oyez.org/cases/2012/12–96 (Accessed 20 June 2019).

24. ". . . upsetting Court decision."—Brinlee, Morgan. "Who Coined Notorious RBG? Here's the History of Ruth Bader Ginsburg's Infamous Nickname." *Bustle.* Created 18 November 2018. https: //www.bustle.com/p/who-coined-notorious-rbg-heres-the-history -of-ruth-bader-ginsburgs-infamous-nickname-13163770 (Accessed 31 May 2019).

25. ". . . as gifts."—Brinlee, Morgan. "Who Coined Notorious RBG? Here's the History of Ruth Bader Ginsburg's Infamous Nickname." *Bustle.* Created 18 November 2018. https://www.bustle.com/p /who-coined-notorious-rbg-heres-the-history-of-ruth-bader-gins burgs-infamous-nickname-13163770 (Accessed 31 May 2019).

26. ". . . end of the 2007 term."—Carmon, Irin, and Knizhnik, Shana. *Notorious RBG: The Life and Times of Ruth Bader Ginsburg.* Pg. 140. New York: Harper Collins, 2015.

27. ". . . democratic responsibility."—Manning-Schaffel, Vivian. "How to dissent like RBG." *NBC News.* Created 10 June 2018. https: //www.nbcnews.com/better/pop-culture/how-dissent-rbg-ncna 881316 (Accessed May 22, 2019).

28. ". . . opinion piece."—Ginsburg, Ruth Bader. "Ruth Bader Ginsburg's Advice for Living." *New York Times.* Created 1 October 2016. https://www.nytimes.com/2016/10/02/opinion/sunday/ruth-bader -ginsburgs-advice-for-living.html (Accessed 22 May 2019).

29. ". . . Court's decision."—Guinier, Lani. "Demosprudence through Dissent" in *The Legacy of Ruth Bader Ginsburg,* ed. Scott Dodson. Pg. 211. (New York: Cambridge University Press, 2015), 206–216.

30. ". . . potato kugel."—Lithwick, Dahlia. "Justice LOLZ Grumpycat Notorious R.B.G." *Slate.* Created 16 March 2015. https://slate .com/human-interest/2015/03/notorious-r-b-g-history-the-origins -and-meaning-of-ruth-bader-ginsburgs-badass-internet-meme.html (Accessed 31 May 2019).

31. ". . . into a minefield."—"Burwell v. Hobby Lobby Stores." Oyez. https://www.oyez.org/cases/2013/13–354 (Accessed June 21, 2019).

32. ". . . politically authoritative women."—Lithwick, Dahlia. "Justice LOLZ Grumpycat Notorious R.B.G." *Slate.* Created 16 March

2015. https://slate.com/human-interest/2015/03/notorious-r-b-g
-history-the-origins-and-meaning-of-ruth-bader-ginsburgs-badass
-internet-meme.html (Accessed 31 May 2019).

33. ". . . in New Republic."—Traister, Rebecca. "How Ruth Bader
Ginsburg Became the Most Popular Woman on the Internet." *New
Republic.* Created 10 July 2014. https://newrepublic.com/article
/118641/ruth-bader-ginsburg-memes-how-internet-fell-love-her
(Accessed 31 May 2019).

34. ". . . legal basis."—Ginsburg, Ruth Bader; Hartnett, Mary; Williams,
Wendy W. *My Own Words.* Pg. 237. New York: Simon & Schuster,
2016.

35. ". . . be settled right."—Ginsburg, Ruth Bader; Hartnett, Mary;
Williams, Wendy W. *My Own Words.* Pg. 286. New York: Simon &
Schuster, 2016.

36. ". . . really necessary."—Ginsburg, Ruth Bader; Hartnett, Mary;
Williams, Wendy W. *My Own Words.* Pg. 280. New York: Simon &
Schuster, 2016.

37. ". . . each justice felt."—Ginsburg, Ruth Bader; Hartnett, Mary;
Williams, Wendy W. *My Own Words.* Pg. 280. New York: Simon &
Schuster, 2016.

38. ". . . improve an opinion," and ". . . justices is helpful."—Ginsburg,
Ruth Bader; Hartnett, Mary; Williams, Wendy W. *My Own Words.*
Pg. 212. New York: Simon & Schuster, 2016.

39. ". . . refine and clarify."—Ginsburg, Ruth Bader; Hartnett, Mary;
Williams, Wendy W. *My Own Words.* Pg. 280–81. New York: Simon
& Schuster, 2016.

40. ". . . ain't over," and ". . . then the public."—Biskupic, Joan.
"Exclusive: Justice Ginsburg shurgs off a rib injury." Reuters. Created
8 August 2012. https://www.reuters.com/article/us-usa-court
-ginsburg/exclusive-justice-ginsburg-shrugs-off-rib-injury-idUS
BRE87801920120809 (Accessed 21 June 2019).

41. ". . . ever the optimist."—Ginsburg, Ruth Bader; Hartnett, Mary;
Williams, Wendy W. *My Own Words.* Pg. 282. New York: Simon &
Schuster, 2016.

42. ". . . important matters are at stake."—Ginsburg, Ruth Bader;
Hartnett, Mary; Williams, Wendy W. *My Own Words.* Pg. 286. New
York: Simon & Schuster, 2016.

Chapter 9: On Creating Change and a Legacy

1. ". . . always be Bubbie."—Spera, Clara. "Ruth Bader Ginsburg's Granddaughter: 'You Know Her as the Notorious RBG, but She's Bubbie to Me.'" *Glamour.* Created 4 May 2018. https://www .glamour.com/story/ruth-bader-ginsburg-granddaughter-bubbie -to-me (Accessed 31 May 2019).

2. ". . . drafty mind."—Dodson, Scott. "Ginsburg, Optimism, and Conflict Management" in *The Legacy of Ruth Bader Ginsburg,* ed. Scott Dodson. Pg. 233. (New York: Cambridge University Press, 2015), 233–236.

3. ". . . women truly be free."—Toobin, Jeffrey and Harlow, Poppy. "Dissenter" in *RBG: Beyond Notorious.* CNN. 6:15. Created 20 August 2018. https://podcasts.apple.com/us/podcast/rbg-beyond -notorious/id1424366161 (Accessed 31 May 2019).

4. ". . . what is in her heart," and ". . . not simply the powerful."— Ginsburg, Ruth Bader; Hartnett, Mary; Williams, Wendy W. *My Own Words.* Pg. 173–174. New York: Simon & Schuster, 2016.

5. ". . . raise their kids."—Williams, Joan. "Beyond the Tough Guise: Justice Ginsburg's Reconstructive Feminism" in *The Legacy of Ruth Bader Ginsburg,* ed. Scott Dodson. Pg. 63. (New York: Cambridge University Press, 2015).

6. Susan Deller Ross quote and info.—Toobin, Jeffrey. "Heavyweight: How Ruth Bader Ginsburg has moved the Supreme Court." *The New Yorker.* Created 11 March 2013. https://www.newyorker.com/mag azine/2013/03/11/heavyweight-ruth-bader-ginsburg (Accessed May 31, 2019).

7. ". . . and now Justice Ruth Bader Ginsburg."—Campbell, Amy Leigh. "Raising the Bar: Ruth Bader Ginsburg and the ACLU Women's Rights Project." *Texas Journal of Women and the Law* 11, p.241. Created 20 March 2003.

8. ". . . woman to be on the Supreme Court" and ". . . ball for women."—Toobin, Jeffrey and Harlow, Poppy. "Her Origins," *RBG: Beyond Notorious.* CNN. 22:16 to 23:02. Created 24 August 2018. https://podcasts.apple.com/us/podcast/rbg-beyond-notorious /id1424366161 (Accessed 31 May 2019).

9. ". . . will go down as a great Justice."—Toobin, Jeffrey and Harlow, Poppy. "Her Origins," *RBG: Beyond Notorious.* CNN. 23:10 to 23:32. Created 24 August 2018. https://podcasts.apple.com/us

/podcast/rbg-beyond-notorious/id1424366161 (Accessed 31 May 2019).

10. "... thirty-five years on the court."—Ginsburg, Ruth Bader; Hartnett, Mary; Williams, Wendy W. *My Own Words*. Pg. 331. New York: Simon & Schuster, 2016.

11. ". . . significant part of her legacy."—Toobin, Jeffrey and Harlow, Poppy. "Her Origins," *RBG: Beyond Notorious*. 39:35. CNN. Created 24 August 2018. https://podcasts.apple.com/us/podcast /rbg-beyond-notorious/id1424366161 (Accessed 31 May 2019).

12. ". . . male liberal judges step down."—Harris, Mary and Lithwick, Dahlia. "Why Ruth Bader Ginsburg Didn't Retire During Obama's Presidency." *Slate*. Created 18 January 2019. https://slate.com /news-and-politics/2019/01/why-rbg-did-not-retire-obama-presidency .html (Accessed 31 May 2019).

13. ". . . vote the way she does."—Toobin, Jeffrey and Harlow, Poppy. "Her Origins" in *RBG: Beyond Notorious*. 38:30. CNN. Created 24 August 2018. https://podcasts.apple.com/us/podcast/rbg -beyond-notorious/id1424366161 (Accessed 31 May 2019).

14. ". . . equipped" and "full-steam."—Ginsburg, Ruth Bader; Hartnett, Mary; Williams, Wendy W. *My Own Words*. Pg. 333. New York: Simon & Schuster, 2016.

15. ". . . relate to."—Longoria, Julia" Sex Appeal," Radiolab, WNYC Studios. Created 23 November 2017. Transcript online. https:// www.wnyc studios.org/story/sex-appeal (Accessed 10 May 2019).

16. "... women's rights field."—"ACLU History: A Decade of Landmarks for Women." ACLU. Created 1 September 2010. https://www.aclu .org/other/aclu-history-decade-landmarks-women (Accessed 31 May 2019).

17. ". . . try to leave tracks."—Ginsburg, Ruth Bader; Hartnett, Mary; Williams, Wendy W. *My Own Words*. Pg. 275. New York: Simon & Schuster, 2016.

18. ". . . a lot."—Carmon, Irin, and Knizhnik, Shana. *Notorious RBG: The Life and Times of Ruth Bader Ginsburg*. Page 180. New York: Harper Collins, 2015.

19. ". . . loyal and generous."—Lan, Lin. "Ruth Bader Ginsburg: Without Precedent." *The Low Down*. Created 6 October 2016. https: //thelowdown.alumni.columbia.edu/ruth_bader_ginsburg_on _columbia (Accessed 31 May 2019).

20. ". . . simple pleasures of life."—Katzmann, Robert. "Reflections on the Confirmation Journey of Ruth Bader Ginsburg, Summer 1993." in *The Legacy of Ruth Bader Ginsburg,* ed. Scott Dodson. Pg. 204. (New York: Cambridge University Press, 2015), 199–205.

21. ". . . three sons."—Toobin, Jeffrey. "Heavyweight: How Ruth Bader Ginsburg has moved the Supreme Court." *The New Yorker.* Created 11 March 2013. https://www.newyorker.com/magazine/2013/03/11 /heavyweight-ruth-bader-ginsburg (Accessed May 31, 2019).

22. ". . . rewrite them."—Shen, Fonda. "Professor Jane Ginsburg reflects on her family history as 'On the Basis of Sex' screens at Athena Film Festival." *Columbia Spectator.* Created 5 March 2019. https: //www.columbiaspectator.com/arts-and-entertainment/2019/03/05 /professor-jane-ginsburg-reflects-on-her-family-history-as-on-the -basis-of-sex-screens-at-athena-film-festival/ (Accessed 31 May 2019).

23. ". . . a family enterprise."—Shen, Fonda. "Professor Jane Ginsburg reflects on her family history as 'On the Basis of Sex' screens at Athena Film Festival." *Columbia Spectator.* Created 5 March 2019. https: //www.columbiaspectator.com/arts-and-entertainment/2019/03/05 /professor-jane-ginsburg-reflects-on-her-family-history-as-on-the -basis-of-sex-screens-at-athena-film-festival/ (Accessed 31 May 2019).

24. ". . . freezer with meals."—Shen, Fonda. "Professor Jane Ginsburg reflects on her family history as 'On the Basis of Sex' screens at Athena Film Festival." *Columbia Spectator.* Created 5 March 2019. https: //www.columbiaspectator.com/arts-and-entertainment/2019/03/05 /professor-jane-ginsburg-reflects-on-her-family-history-as-on-the -basis-of-sex-screens-at-athena-film-festival/ (Accessed 31 May 2019).

25. ". . . breastfeeding a baby."—De Hart, Jane Sherron. *Ruth Bader Ginsburg.* Pg. 163. New York: Alfred A. Knopf, Penguin Random House, 2018.

26. ". . . nephew's wedding."—Schulman, Michael. "Ruth Bader Ginsburg's Nephew on Winning the Aunt Lottery." *The New Yorker.* Created 17 December 2018. https://www.newyorker.com/magazine /2018/12/24/ruth-bader-ginsburgs-nephew-on-winning-the-aunt -lottery (Accessed 31 May 2019).

27. ". . . Kahn and Mitchem."—Dowd, Maureen. "Presiding at Same-Sex Wedding, Ruth Bader Ginsburg Emphasizes the Word 'Constitution.'" *New York Times.* Created 18 May 2015. https: //www.nytimes.com/politics/first-draft/2015/05/18/presiding

-at-same-sex-wedding-ruth-bader-ginsburg-emphasizes-a-key
-word/ (Accessed 31 May 2019).

28. ". . . have a new baby"—Carmon, Irin, and Knizhnik, Shana. *Notorious RBG: The Life and Times of Ruth Bader Ginsburg.* Pg. 124. New York: Harper Collins, 2015.

29. ". . . authors revealed."—Carmon, Irin, and Knizhnik, Shana. *Notorious RBG: The Life and Times of Ruth Bader Ginsburg.* Pg. 125. New York: Harper Collins, 2015.

30. ". . . traveling performance."—Carmon, Irin, and Knizhnik, Shana. *Notorious RBG: The Life and Times of Ruth Bader Ginsburg.* Page 167. New York: Harper Collins, 2015.

31. ". . . recitals at the court."—Carmon, Irin, and Knizhnik, Shana. *Notorious RBG: The Life and Times of Ruth Bader Ginsburg.* Page 167. New York: Harper Collins, 2015.

32. ". . . opera recordings" and "exercise to that noise."—The Late Show with Stephen Colbert. "Stephen Works out With Ruth Bader Ginsburg." Posted 21 March 2018. https://www.youtube.com/watch?v=0oBodJHX1Vg (Accessed 31 May 2019).

33. ". . . would never do that."—de Vogue, Ariane. "Ginsburg and Scalia on parasailing, elephants and not being '100% sober.'" CNN. Created 13 February 2015. https://www.cnn.com/2015/02/13/politics/ginsburg-scalia-parasailing-sotu-wine/ (Accessed 31 May 2019).

34. ". . . parsimonious entries."—Lithwick, Dahlia. "*RBG* Reveals the Woman Behind the Memes." *Slate.* Created 30 April 2018. https://slate.com/culture/2018/04/rbg-the-new-documentary-reviewed.html (Accessed 1 June 2019).

35. ". . . marvelously funny."—Barnes, Robert. "The new film *RBG* reveals how Ruth Bader Ginsburg became a meme—and why that's so surprising." *Washington Post.* Created 3 March 2018. https://www.washingtonpost.com/lifestyle/the-new-film-rbg-reveals-ruth-bader-ginsburgs-life-before-she-became-a-meme/2018/05/03/794a881a-4c9f-11e8-af46-b1d6dc0d9bfe_story.html?utm_term=.11bd9599faaa (Accessed 1 June 2019).

36. ". . . gallows humor."—Totenberg, Nina. "Notes on a Life" in *The Legacy of Ruth Bader Ginsburg,* ed. Scott Dodson. Pg. 4. (New York: Cambridge University Press, 2015), 3–12.

37. ". . . support in child rearing."—Carmon, Irin, and Knizhnik, Shana. *Notorious RBG: The Life and Times of Ruth Bader Ginsburg*. Page 114. New York: Harper Collins, 2015.

38. ". . . climate of the era."—Ginsburg, Ruth Bader; Hartnett, Mary; Williams, Wendy W. *My Own Words*. Pg. 161. New York: Simon & Schuster, 2016.

39. ". . . she writes."—Lapidus, Lenor M., Luthra, Namita, and Martin, Emily. "Celebrating Thirty Years: Women's Rights Project Annual Report 2001." *ACLU*. Pg. 9. Created December 2001.

40. "decades of challenges" and ". . . too much too soon" and "pressure on lawmakers."—Campbell, Amy Leigh. "Raising the Bar: Ruth Bader Ginsburg and the ACLU Women's Rights Project." 11 Texas Journal of Women and the Law. Pg. 157. Created 20 March 2003.

41. ". . . things needed to change."—Williams, Joan C., and Ginsburg, Ruth Bader. "Conversation with Justice Ginsburg." C-SPAN. Created 15 September 2011. https://www.c-span.org/video/?301560–1 /conversation-justice-ginsburg (Accessed 31 May 2019).

42. ". . . generation prior."—Hockenberry, John. "Transcript: Interview with Supreme Court Justice Ruth Bader Ginsburg." *PRI's The World*. Created 16 September 2013. https://www.pri .org/stories/2013-09-16/transcript-interview-supreme-court-justice -ruth-bader-ginsburg (Accessed 31 May 2019).

43. ". . . state by state."—Hirsham, Linda. *Sisters in Law*. Pg. 81. New York: HarperCollins, 2015.

44. ". . . with this critique."—Waxman, Olivia B. "Ruth Bader Ginsburg Wishes This Case Had Legalized Abortion Instead of *Roe v. Wade*." *Time*. Created 2 August 2018. https://time.com/5354490 /ruth-bader-ginsburg-roe-v-wade/ (Accessed 19 June 2019).

45. ". . . feedback loop."—Williams, Joan C., and Ginsburg, Ruth Bader. "Conversation with Justice Ginsburg." C-SPAN. Created 15 September 2011. https://www.c-span.org/video/?301560–1/conver sation-justice-ginsburg (Accessed 31 May 2019).

46. Goals at ACLU.—Williams, Joan C., and Ginsburg, Ruth Bader. "Conversation with Justice Ginsburg." C-SPAN. Created 15 September 2011. https://www.c-span.org/video/?301560–1/conversation-justice -ginsburg (Accessed 31 May 2019).

47. ". . . cases not yet seen."—Nomination of Ruth Bader Ginsburg, to be Associate Justice of the Supreme Court of the United States.

Committee on the Judiciary. Pg. 50. Washington: US Government Printing Office, 1994.

48. ". . . cancer surgery."—McCluskey, Megan. "People Promptly Offer Bones of Their Own After Ruth Bader Ginsburg Fractures Her Ribs." *TIME.* Created 8 November 2018. http://time.com/5449074/ruth -bader-ginsburg-broken-ribs/ (Accessed May 24, 2019).

49. ". . . role in judicial decisions."—De Hart, Jane Sherron. *Ruth Bader Ginsburg.* Pg. 173. New York: Alfred A. Knopf, Penguin Random House, 2018.

50. ". . . ever enlarged group."—Carmon, Irin, and Knizhnik, Shana. *Notorious RBG: The Life and Times of Ruth Bader Ginsburg.* Page 176. New York: Harper Collins, 2015.

51. ". . . is seldom linear."—De Hart, Jane Sherron. *Ruth Bader Ginsburg.* Pg. 475. New York: Alfred A. Knopf, Penguin Random House, 2018.

52. When she presided over naturalization ceremony.—De Hart, Jane Sherron. *Ruth Bader Ginsburg.* Pg. 531. New York: Alfred A. Knopf, Penguin Random House, 2018.

53. ". . . whatever ability she has."—Carmon, Irin, and Knizhnik, Shana. *Notorious RBG: The Life and Times of Ruth Bader Ginsburg.* Page 169. New York: Harper Collins, 2015.

Index